REJECTING REJECTION

How To Take Control Of Your Life In Uncontrollable Times

BETTE PRICE

KENDALL/HUNT PUBLISHING COMPANY
4050 Westmark Drive Dubuque, Iowa 52002

ISBN 0-7872-2681-5

Printed in the United States of America
10 9 8 7 6 5 4 3 2 1

▼ Dedication ▼

To my husband John, whose love, belief, patience, and encouragement supported my dream of writing this book, and, to my two phenomenal children, Lani and Blake, who are my greatest treasures.

For Kay –
Here's to many memorable moments!
Bette Price

▼ Contents ▼

▼ Acknowledgments ▼

From the moment I began thinking and talking about writing this book, I have been blessed with wonderful people who have encouraged me, been patient with me and lovingly prodded me when I needed it.

My husband John continues to be my greatest support, never losing patience, always applauding my vision and helping tremendously by being the greatest detail man in the world. And, I'm blessed with the pride of my children, Lani and Blake, who are the light of my life and the base of my passion and purpose.

Jan Hamill has been my number one support from the start, nudging me gently to set a deadline and get it done and always there when I needed someone with whom to talk things through. Candace Smallwood supported from afar, checking long distance every step of the way with encouragement, objectivity and honest feedback. Barbara Glanz shared her publishing wisdom and put me in her prayers. Pud Kearns kept telling me to do it, since she finished her book, she knew I could too.

Jane Handly was my first mentor in my speaking career, and early on she urged me to share my story. Dave Gorden convinced me that even corporate America could learn from my journey. Judith Briles opened doors and helped me to brainstorm. Lisa Kanarek helped organize my office so I could work efficiently.

Alva Goodall, Noreen Whalen, and Ruth Martin gave me the love and support that only long-time, knowing friends can provide. DeLene Gilbert, Dianne Ogle and Vicki Turner were new friends who jumped on the bandwagon of support from the moment I met them. Cherl Jensen was my dose of enthusiasm whenever I needed it. Dr. Joy Bodzioch, my friend, associate and psychological resource, was instrumental in numerous ways.

A special thanks to Linda Hansen who, despite her serious corporate nature, convinced me there was a great need for sharing my story to help deal with mounting human development issues.

One very special woman helped me keep my sense of humor at discouraging times, talked with me daily when I was in town, and reached out with love like I was her own — my mother-in-law, Mary Margaret Price.

Larry TenBrink of Shoestring Advertising rescued me when I needed artistic help, and his art director, Sharon Traverse, designed a book cover that captured in art form, the vitality and life I envisioned for this book. And, Lucille Enix, the best editor in the world, not only put the finishing touches to every chapter, but thoroughly thrilled me with the excitement she expressed for the book.

Finally, I want to send a special prayer of thanks to my grandfather who has always been my guiding angel.

▼ Introduction ▼

This is a book that has evolved from my personal experiences, written for you with the sole purpose of sharing a process that has brought more purpose, balance, zest and control to my own life, in the hope that it will help you to achieve the same balance and control in your life. It has been said that nothing is new, merely what you bring to it. What I bring to this book is a perspective that reflects first-hand knowledge of reclaiming control of my life along with the experiences of others who have shared their challenges and triumphs as well. The principles and action steps are offered as guidelines. Some will present ideal solutions; others may merely ignite your thought process. Embrace those for which you are ready. Hold the others in reserve for later.

Although I do not have a degree in psychology or human behavior, I am an expert on dealing with rejection having lived with it from birth. As a result I have studied extensively and have experienced first-hand the power of reestablishing self-worth and regaining control of one's own life.

My own experience has shown me that one's ability to effectively cope with rejection is at the core of effectively dealing with such losses as job, position, and status as well as such personal issues as broken marriages, loss of loved ones, aging and various forms of discrimination. Increasingly, one's ability to cope with rejection has been tested. Professionals have lived through the mass purging of America's workforce, the by-product of mergers, take-overs, reorganizations, downsizing and so-called right-sizing. Failure to recognize the powerful role rejection plays in our ability to cope often results in misplaced blame, low self-esteem, and unrealistic expectations of how to rebuild our future.

My own inability to take control of my life stemmed from an unconscious denial. I considered myself a survivor—optimistic, stoic, always ready to pick myself up and start all over again. Friends and colleagues seemed to admire my ability to hurdle adversities. I wore tenacity like a merit badge! Outwardly my life appeared ideal— colleagues saw me as strong, confident, and successful. Suggesting that I could not achieve something I aspired to, merely motivated me to prove that I could. Without a teaching degree I was hired to teach professional development and speech for a junior college of business. I was so successful that a major educational publisher hired me to do special teacher training programs to help implement their text books into the classroom. When my husband was transferred to Cleveland, Ohio, I followed the suggestion of one of the publishing executives and sought a career in television. Although I had no formal training, I broke into a top ten television market within one year and shortly thereafter was named co-hostess of my own news and information show.

When forced to move again, I met the challenge by creating a management position for myself at the convention and visitors bureau in a city about to host the Republican National Convention. I built from scratch a public relations department and produced and scripted a promotional audio-visual presentation that was presented to organizations throughout the nation. From this success I re-launched a television career, co-hosting a daily talk show. One year later, without a journalism degree, I was hired by a major newspaper to be society editor. Besides writing a twice-weekly, widely read column, I wrote features, profiles and an occasional news story. I "scooped" the sports staff with a Sunday, front-page, copyright story and landed an exclusive story on Richard Bloch's personal struggle to survive lung cancer. The copyright story about H & R Bloch's co-founder was picked up by the wire services world wide. Later I contributed to the team coverage of the tragic Hyatt Hotel sky walk collapse, overall coverage earned the newspaper a Pulitzer Prize.

So what was the problem?

It was never enough. My life was totally out of control. I had no balance. My role in life had become my whole life.

Relationships were strained. Increasingly I felt stressed, overly aggressive, unfulfilled, even rejected. But, I denied it. Stoically I forged onward, creating the next deal, making things happen, thinking each new achievement was the answer. Then, one day, I was forced to confront reality. I encountered my ultimate rejection.

As a child, mother had left me to be raised by my grandparents. When it was convenient, she and my father would visit or I would be flown to New York, where they lived, to spend the summer. Then I'd return to grandma's which I considered my real home. The arrangement made for a strange childhood; one that failed to create the normal bond between mother and child.

As an adult, I experienced many strained times with mother. On numerous occasions she refused my phone calls, admonished me with hostile letters or bluntly told me she wanted nothing to do with me. She and my father eventually retired to Florida; my daughter and her family had moved nearby and I planned a trip to visit them. I decided I would attempt to reunite with mother as part of the visit. I was convinced that at this stage in life we could come to some positive resolve. I was excited and hopeful when she agreed to meet with me. However, when I got there and called her, I found she had changed her mind. "I don't know what it is you wanted to talk about," she said, " but I feel I have had to make choices in my life and I don't have room for you." With little else said, she hung up the phone. There was such finality in her voice.

This incredibly painful experience became, in reality, a gift. It forced me to recognize that for many years I had allowed circumstances, people, jobs and events to take control of my life. Consciously or unconsciously I had made that choice. Now, if I was to regain control of my life, I had to make different choices.

This turning point led me on a quest for new knowledge. I began researching the work of psychologists and other professionals in the field of behavior. I talked with various experts, consulted with a minister and read every popular or clinical book I could get my hands on that explored everything from co-dependency to healing the inner child. Many were blame-based, and conflicted with my beliefs and values. Others gave valuable insights and heightened my understanding and awareness. I eventually concluded that I, like many individuals, regardless of gender, background, ethnicity or economics, did not necessarily see myself as afflicted or co-dependent or in need of analysis or therapy. If I were to gain control of my life, I merely needed an understanding and a process. That is what this book is about.

I have concluded that there are three Powerful Principles that guide us in taking control of our lives. Within each principle, I have identified four action steps which I call Price Points of Action. Each is an action that I have personally implemented in my own life. Each is an action that I continually revisit and focus on to keep my life in balance. Each is an action that helps me to respond positively to the uncertainties and change that are ever present in today's quest for balance, success and fulfillment.

The principles, tactics and strategies presented in *Rejecting Rejection* in no way profess to replace professional psychological help, nor do they promise a quick fix. *Rejecting Rejection* does, however, provide inspiration, guidance, hope and practical proven strategies that will enable you to recognize the integral part rejection plays in determining how you respond to life's challenges. *Rejecting Rejection* also gives you responsible action steps for regaining control of your life. While your situation may vary from mine, the principles and action steps that grew from my own shift in thinking can be easily applied to your situation. They are principles and action steps that are as meaningful to today's leaders and managers as to individuals who are reshaping their own new futures.

As you read *Rejecting Rejection,* you will find that regardless of obstacles others set before you, you have within you a powerful ability to take control of your life and create new successes for the rest of your life. As you regain control of your life, you will find that you will begin to achieve a greater power than any position, title or income has ever been able to provide for you. If you learn and practice the techniques and skills presented throughout this book, you will follow a process that will help you to recognize the important difference between "who" you are and "what" you are. As a result you will...

1. become mentally and emotionally capable of dealing with rejection without taking it personally;

2. increase your ability to communicate effectively when responding to rejections;

3. strengthen your coping skills;

4. find an inner strength that will help you to make more rational decisions;

5. express your true self more clearly, and

6. take control of your life during these ever-changing, uncertain and uncontrollable times.

I know this can work for you, because it has worked for me.

CHAPTER 1

Balance Your Power

PRINCIPLE #1

Balance the Power You Give to External Conditions with the Power You Give to Internal Feelings, Beliefs and Knowledge

One of my earliest recollections of an external force creating a seemingly uncontrollable situation, was when I was a flight attendant for Northwest Orient Airlines. A popular schedule for which my roommate and I would frequently bid was called a "shuttle." It encompassed multiple destinations over a period of one week and quickly accumulated many flight hours, giving us back-to-back days off each month. We would fly from our home base of Minneapolis to Miami, then to New York City, Seattle and back to Minneapolis. In each city we would have ample layover time for resting, shopping, visiting friends and whatever else we wanted to do. As part of this monthly schedule, we would also work a couple of quick "turn-around flights," which meant that on one or two nights that month we would also fly from Minneapolis to Chicago and back again.

One day, before beginning our week-long shuttle, my roommate and I were returning from an afternoon of shopping. On the car radio we heard that a Northwest Airlines flight had crashed outside Tell City, Indiana. It was our flight, one day before we were scheduled to fly it. You might imagine our dismay and shock.

The next day we reported to work with a fair amount of trepidation and concern. All that airline personnel knew at that point was that the fatal flight had encountered clear air turbulence on what otherwise seemed like a beautiful, clear day. Later it would be determined that there was a flaw in the design of the prop-jet aircraft—not enough suspension in its wings. When the aircraft encountered severe turbulence, the force literally snapped off the wings and the aircraft plummeted to the earth, killing everyone on board.

As you have probably discerned, our flight that day after the crash went fine. As the next few weeks went by without incident, we began to set our apprehensions aside. We had little concern the night we reported for one of the turn-around flights to Chicago and back. Our captain, a man named Larry Abbey, has the only name I've ever remembered from my entire flight career. Captain Abbey was a serious sort of fellow. He rarely dined with the rest of the crew and was known to be rather quiet, reserved and cautious. Behind his back, some of the crew members referred to him as "chicken Larry Abbey," because of his cautious nature.

The flight to Chicago was smooth until we neared our final approach. For a few moments we encountered some mild turbulence—nothing major. Once on the ground, the crew exchanged a few passing comments about flying through turbulence in the same type of aircraft that had been downed.

Before passengers boarded for the return flight, Captain Abbey called us to the cockpit to inform us that radar indicated we might encounter more severe turbulence on our return to Minneapolis. Therefore, he wanted to be sure we checked everyone carefully for secure seat belts and directed us to wait until he called us to begin serving dinner.

Despite his over-cautious reputation, I secured my own seat belt tightly as I prepared for departure. Along with another attendant, I was seated in the tail of the plane in the window position of the flight attendant's jump seat. Soon we were speeding down the runway. As the aircraft began its climb, I gazed at the dazzling array of bright city lights below. It was a crystal clear evening, not a cloud in sight. We began to bank to the right, turning ever-so-slightly. Then suddenly, as if a giant hand had been thrust from the sky to pick up the plane and throw it around, we were tossed and turned in the most intense turbulence I have ever encountered. Pillows flew through the air, a garbage container went shooting down the aisle, dust wafted from the force of passengers being thrust up and down in their seats. I was shaken from side to side with such force that my clothes literally turned on my body. The situation seemed totally uncontrollable.

I remember thinking, "How on earth can the crew maintain any control of this aircraft?" Yet within minutes the situation changed. Suddenly the chaotic tumbling was replaced with calm, smooth movement. The captain announced we would be returning to Chicago. You could hear the sigh of relief when we touched the runway. Although emotionally shaken by the experience, we knew we were safe. We had returned to earth with our wings intact, no major injuries, and tremendous gratitude for "cautious" Captain Abbey and his competent crew.

My purpose in sharing this story with you is that I believe it symbolizes principle number one. The external conditions that night were tumultuous and uncontrollable. There was nothing any mortal being could have done to control the weather conditions. Captain Abbey knew that. Yet by balancing the power that he gave to these uncontrollable conditions with the power he gave to his own internal feeling, beliefs and knowledge, he was able to take a measure of control which enabled him and the crew to stabilize the aircraft and bring us down safely.

I believe that life creates many situations similar to this. We think we're flying along smoothly, everything seems to be going fine, then WHAM, out of nowhere this turmoil grabs us, shakes us up and turns our life around. The turbulence comes in many forms—job loss, position loss, sales loss, management shake-ups, a difficult boss, reorganization of the company, health problems, family problems, marriage problems, and a host of other disappointments or unplanned events. All are external. Most are conditions that we have little control over. Yet, far too often we dwell on the external conditions, allowing them to take control of our lives.

Just as there was nothing Captain Abbey could do to change the external conditions the night of our flight, there is often little we can personally do to alter many of the external conditions that impact our lives. Yet we do have the choice to draw from our internal feelings, beliefs and knowledge in a way that can help us to respond to the conditions with well-balanced decisions and actions.

Balanced decisions and actions require balanced thinking. In order to think in a balanced style, it is important to understand the three ways in which we think.

The Three Dimensions of Thinking

Philosopher and scientist, Dr. Robert S. Hartman, an expert in the field of values, determined that there are three dimensions of value to the way one thinks: Intrinsic, extrinsic and systemic.

- *Intrinsic Thinking.* This dimension of thinking focuses on how we think about ourselves as unique, one-of-a-kind human beings. This includes loving ourself just the way we are, accepting our strengths and weaknesses and being fully accountable for our own actions. How we think about ourselves without comparison to anyone else's criteria, impacts our empathy and self-esteem.

- *Extrinsic Thinking.* This dimension of thinking focuses on practicality and comparisons. It impacts how we view our role performance in comparison to how we think it "should" be performed. This dimension highly impacts our thinking in the arena of business. It impacts such things as how we think about money, status, and social recognition. It determines how we take action to get things done and how we make choices about which is good, better and best. This dimension influences how we compare things and people; one strategy versus another, one individual's style against another's.
- *Systemic Thinking.* This dimension of thinking focuses on structure, order, and right or wrong decisions. It impacts the intensity with which we adhere to laws, contracts, rules, and policies and how we think one "ought" to think or "should" think. This dimension impacts order, logic and the process to be followed as well as acceptable protocol, methods to be adhered to, and punctuality.

Let's say you are responsible for overseeing a male manager. An example of balanced thinking would be:

Genuine concern for his expressed desire for an office with natural sunlight, up-graded computer equipment and programs that are important to his productivity, acceptance of his communication and people strengths, and need for support staff to compensate for his weaknesses, in follow-up and detail (intrinsic) PLUS, an attention to his ability to meet scheduled deadlines, awareness of how he compares to other departmental managers, and evaluating how he is paid in relation to his results and responsibilities, (extrinsic), PLUS attention to how he follows company policy during employee reviews, adheres to company policy regarding vacation and sick leave, fosters the company's mission through his management style and enhances the company's image by dressing appropriately (systemic).

An example of imbalanced thinking regarding this same manager, would be focusing on his strong management style and adherence to company policy, but paying little or no attention to his communication and people strengths or his perceived need for support in follow-up and detail.

No one is perfectly balanced in their thinking. We all have biases that blur our thinking, thus impact the way we come to decisions and behave. What is important is to understand ourselves well enough that we will recognize our biases and learn to make adjustments to create more balance to our thinking and actions.

If we ignore the intrinsic dimension of our thinking, we can tend to ignore an individual's unique value, therefore taking their value and dignity for granted. When we ignore this dimension in how we think about ourself, we become vulnerable to feeling that we are being taken advantage of or unappreciated. We can also feel alone, less a part of the team, or like an odd-man-out. When we ignore this dimension, we devalue our own uniqueness.

When we ignore the extrinsic dimension we fail to acknowledge our competence and our ability to make practical judgments about what is right or wrong, best or worst. Our common sense is devalued, we underestimate our monetary value or need for recognition. Ignoring this dimension diminishes our ability to feel useful to our fullest potential as a contributing member of society.

If the systemic dimension is ignored we fail to value the need for structure, timeliness, laws, regulations or policies, thus we become inefficient at managing our time and can be inattentive to issues such as quality, order, procedures, and clarity. Ignoring this dimension diminishes our loyalty and accountability and impedes our ability to think sequentially or present ideas in a logical (1,2,3) step-by-step pattern.

When imbalances exist, stress develops. It has often been said that a strength overused becomes a weakness. Thus, if we either undervalue or overvalue any one dimension of thinking, we become imbalanced in our thinking and become vulnerable to stress. When this happens, we are more apt to lose control to external conditions.

In the next chapter I have identified four Price Point Action Steps to help you balance your thinking and therefore, help to balance the power you give to external conditions with the power you give to internal feelings, beliefs and knowledge.

CHAPTER 2

Taking Things Personally

There are those who live in rooms of experience that we can never enter.

—John Steinbeck

▼ Price Point of Action 1

Accept What Is without Taking Things Personally

The word "rejection" triggers different memories for different people. Regardless of individual situations, rejection is something you share with many other people. Some take rejections personally, some do not. Think about how you believe the following people took their respective rejections:

Mary lost her job following a poor performance review.

George was denied a promotion he thought he deserved.

Alice found herself suddenly single when her husband found a younger woman and a more fulfilling relationship.

Donald lost his job because management reduced his department.

Margaret was put into a new and different position against her wishes when her company merged and shifted departments.

Mark's parents died, leaving him to be raised by an elderly aunt and uncle.

Mary's status with her peers was diminished when her husband was replaced as president of the division.

Jack was told he'd never succeed because he didn't fit the company mold.

Bill and Jeannie revealed in their singles group how each had been "dumped" by their former lovers.

Nora's Mother committed suicide when Nora was a teenager.

The stories could go on and on, but you understand. The important question to ask is, "Were any of these rejections meant to be personal?"

Now, create your own picture. What comes to mind as a time you personally felt rejection? Stop reading for a moment and, as your memories of rejection come to mind, write them down. They will be useful for you to refer to later.

I felt rejected when....

Did you take this rejection personally? How did you feel about the rejection at the time?

Madelyn's Earliest Memory of Rejection

Madelyn, a woman in her mid-forties who has had two successful careers in the corporate sector and now commands thousands of dollars a day to predict future trends for many major companies, recalls a very early time in her life when she first encountered rejection.

"We weren't poor, but my parents had what I'd call a modest income. My aunt and uncle who were childless were the ones considered to be successful. One day when I was very young, I happened to overhear my mother say, 'If we didn't have Madelyn to raise, we'd be able to do things too'.

"Although I realize now that they weren't blaming me for their economic situation, at the time I believed that I stood in their way of living a life as successful as my aunt and uncle. So, all my life I tried to be the best at everything I did so they would see that I was worth the sacrifice that I believed they had made by having me."

Madelyn took what she heard as a personal rejection, one that impacted the way she approached life for years to come. Her reaction was not uncommon. Madelyn's memories affected her self-esteem, how she valued herself as a person. Her role awareness and self direction were less affected. In fact, she actually overachieved in her roles, becoming a straight "A" student, a college graduate with high honors, a rapidly rising corporate leader and success. She eventually risked making it on her own as an entrepreneurial woman.

Not everyone is so fortunate. All too often rejection affects multiple areas of life; your **self-esteem**, your **role awareness** and your **self-direction**. These three aspects make up your true self. The value you place on each aspect determines how you think about (1) yourself as a unique person, (2) yourself in various roles and in society, and (3) yourself and the rules you have established for what you should do and how you should behave.

Although this area of development will be covered more thoroughly later in this book, it is important to know that how you think in these areas determines how you react to the "no's" in your life, whether they come in the form of broken relationships, lost sales, the denial of a job or promotion, or something as simple as not having your ideas or concepts accepted. Once you become caught in the "No Syndrome," it is easy to repeat the cycle and increasingly take things personally.

The field of sales perhaps presents the greatest example of professional rejection, of being subjected to the "No Syndrome." Those who sell for a living can almost expect rejection as a daily occurrence. Because someone has spent years in the profession of selling, does not imply that they have learned to deal with rejections easily or without taking major rejections personally. My friend Kevin is a perfect example.

Kevin's Story

Kevin is a professional salesman. He's been in sales all of his adult life and is considered extremely successful. One evening I met Kevin and his wife for dinner and during the course of conversation I brought up the subject of rejection and that I was writing this book.

"Rejection!" Kevin exclaimed, "let me tell you about rejection." He described an experience he had had during a sales call several weeks earlier.

After Kevin had talked with the prospective client on the phone several times, the prospect agreed to meet with Kevin. When Kevin arrived for the meeting the prospect greeted him cordially and began to openly respond to Kevin's questions. At times during the discussion, the prospect leaned back in his chair and sometimes he even fully turned away as if distracted by something outside his office. Overall, though, Kevin felt the conversation was moving along fine.

"Then abruptly he changed his attitude," Kevin explained. "He pushed his chair away from his desk, rose to his feet, struck a confident stance, looked me square in the eye and firmly stated, 'I don't like your products, I don't like your company and I want you to leave my office'."

Although this unpleasant incident had happened nearly five weeks earlier, I could readily see that Kevin still felt enraged. The tone of his voice reflected the anger he felt. His pupils narrowed and his brow became furrowed. His tensed expression revealed both the hurt and anger he held on to. Clenching his fist, he leaned forward. "He made me so mad," Kevin said as he restrained himself from hitting the table.

"You took it personally, didn't you?" I asked, wanting to confirm my suspicion.

"You bet I did," Kevin responded adamantly.

His response might not surprise you. It is understandable that you might relate to how he felt at the time — angry, hurt, frustrated, even somewhat embarrassed and stupid — all emotions Kevin confessed to feeling. You might even understand how Kevin initially thought the prospect's outrage was directed at him personally; after all, he was nearly thrown out of the office.

But, was it personal? Did this prospect really dislike Kevin?

With passage of time, a clear mind might judge this situation differently. Yet Kevin continued to believe that the incident was a personal affront. He could not move beyond and consider other factors that might have caused the prospect to react so drastically. Instead, weeks later he chose to continue to carry it as a personal rejection. Kevin was caught up in the "No Syndrome."

When you fail to understand what triggers your reactions to someone else's negative actions, you will continue to react in the same way over and over. The reaction sets up what I call the **Cycle of Rejection**, a process you will learn more about later in this book.

Not every rejection you face will impact you as dramatically as Kevin's encounter, yet many will be enough to create similar emotions if you have not learned how to effectively deal with rejection.

People can reject your ideas, your concepts, your attention, even your love. They can reject you because of your color, your age, your education, your background, your nationality, your beliefs or various and sundry other things. However, your ability to cope will determine its impact.

Today, psychologists believe that some evidence suggests that rejection hurts more than it did a decade or so ago. As a result, it is becoming more and more difficult to reject the fear of rejection. Not dealing with rejection effectively takes a mental toll. Inevitably self esteem plummets. To minimize the hurt, many people simply avoid dealing with rejection by denying it. Research, however, suggests that this is not the most effective approach. In fact, I have found that the longer one denies one's feelings of rejection, the more damaging the results can be. And, the more likely it is to be taken personally.

Ruth's Rejection

When Ruth became disenchanted with her secretarial job, she talked about getting a new job. She interviewed for a few. But, the rejections nearly overwhelmed her. For more than a year Ruth convinced herself that because she did not have the college degrees stipulated for many of the positions that attracted her, she would be rejected. This became a very personal issue that severely eroded her confidence.

One day I called Ruth to tell her about a position in non-profit that I thought she was ideally suited for. She had personalized all her previous rejections so dramatically that she could barely picture herself fulfilling the role. As we talked more extensively and I encouraged her to take credit for some of her abilities, she finally acknowledged that many of the aspects required for this position were things she had experienced and accomplished quite successfully.

Finally, Ruth decided to interview for the job. Much to her own amazement, she was hired. In the years since, Ruth has grown tremendously, particularly with respect to how she responds to perceived rejections. Eventually she became the executive director for a major health-related non-profit, a position which required an applicant's Masters Degree and extensive experience. Despite Ruth's lack of either, she aggressively pursued the position and was eventually considered to be the best candidate. In her new role she used her previous work-related knowledge and know-how to implement a plan that pulled the organization out of debt, expanded its programs and strengthened its community leadership and funding. Through self-education, determination and the confidence to select qualified and competent staff members, Ruth has continued to prove to herself, and a supportive board of directors, a whole new level of confidence and esteem.

Ruth is a product of our times. She grew up in a generation where women were not encouraged to continue their education nor to achieve. It took extraordinary effort on her part to believe she could move beyond her previously self-imposed limitations. "Once I realized that I was the one who had personalized many of the rejections I experienced, I recognized that how I chose to respond to those rejections was critical to what happened next," Ruth says. "I guess I never realized that I had a choice."

Both Ruth and Kevin responded to experiences that they perceived as personal rejections in ways that they had become accustomed to. That made it easy to place blame.

Kevin concluded that he lost the sale because the prospect didn't like him. This judgment provided an excuse for losing the sale, but it did not provide a resolution. Ruth concluded she wasn't hired for several jobs because the employers didn't think she was qualified. Again, this thinking provided an excuse, but no resolution. As a result, each person carried the anger and disappointment for long periods of time.

It is easy to think that the hurt and anger will eventually go away. In reality the negative emotions merely become suppressed, only to resurface the next time the person encounters rejection. Like a cresting wave, emotional reactions build with intensity. Bit-by-bit, instance-by-instance, the person forms a belief system that says all rejections are personal. Eventually, either consciously or unconsciously, they continue to react to the "No Syndrome."

The "No Syndrome" as a Driver

Sometimes rejection actually becomes the impetus to pursue greater achievements, to spur you on by an "I'll show you" attitude. As a result, some people who appear successful often go through life disguising their lack of ability to deal with rejection by overachieving in their quest for acceptance and true fulfillment. Because these people are frequently able to accomplish financial success or positions of status, they give an appearance of being confident, stable and secure. What has happened is they have become driven not so much by ambition but by their need to find some immediate sense of satisfaction.

Often these individuals move from one success to another, easily bored and constantly seeming to need new challenges. In some respects they drive right over rejections, ignoring them in hope that the feelings of emptiness deep inside will go away. These are people who, regardless of their external image, often feel frustrated and unfulfilled on the inside. This frustration frequently manifests itself in broken relationships, pretentious displays of affluence, substance abuse and an insatiable quest for what they perceive as power. These are people whose lives lack balance. They don't feel acceptance for who they are but rather for how they have performed in their work and societal roles. These people often achieve worldly success at the sacrifice of a balanced, whole life.

John R. O'Neil, author of *The Paradox of Success,* writes about individuals consumed by achieving that, "their bodies go home every night, but psychologically and spiritually they remain imprisoned by the roles they have worked so hard to construct for themselves."[1]

When we hear that people have it all, O'Neil writes, we should be concerned for them. The price paid for having it all is incalculable; no walks in the park, no spontaneous plans to catch a movie, not time to bounce a chid or play a quick set of tennis with a friend.[2]

Rejection for these people becomes extremely personal.

---

[1] The Paradox of Success, John R. O'Neil, Tarcher/Putnam, p. 24

[2] The Paradox of Success, John R. O'Neil, Tarcher/Putnam, p. 113

David. He Appears to Have It All

A young businessman, who we will refer to as David, has been proving his worth through achievements nearly all of his 35 years. Only recently has he begun to admit the lack of fulfillment he feels despite his appearance of success.

David is an only child. His parents began the family business several years before David's birth and have built it into a multi-million dollar success. David joined the family business several years ago only after imprinting his own style in the corporate world. He's worked hard to contribute to the growth of the family business, taken an active place in the community, and served on numerous boards and committees. He is perceived by most of his contemporaries as a business and civic leader but has also earned a reputation for being overly sensitive.

"Sometimes it's a real juggling act working with David," a colleague of his once told me. "You have to approach him like walking on eggs; he just takes everything so personally."

I knew what he meant; I'd seen it myself. Sometimes the slightest comment hurt his feelings. Typically, after a few days, David would begin explaining his behavior and over-justifying his actions. Clearly he felt guilty. Sometimes he tried to rectify his actions by buying lavish gifts for those he had annoyed. Then, as if to prove that he was still in control, he would take on some new task to achieve. Trying to maintain either a business or personal relationship with David was often like walking a tight rope.

Through the years that I have known David I have seen his behavior begin to take an incredible toll. Despite his confident public posture, he has overindulged in food to the point his weight has begun to impact his health. His irrational outbursts have driven away some of the people he claims to care for most. Even his children show signs of the stress in their own behaviors. David's behavior has become critical, negative and immature. Only lately has he hurt deeply enough to begin to look at why he feels no personal gratification. He's beginning to admit feeling that the company was more important to his parents than he was; perhaps his earliest feelings of rejection.

Each of the individuals you have read about is an ideal example of taking rejections personally. Recognizing and understanding the Cycle of Rejection is an important step in realizing that most rejections are not meant as personal. You will learn more about this cycle in the following chapters.

When we take rejections personally, we create an imbalance in the power that we give to external forces such as the corporation that down-sized, the boss who terminated us, the colleague who disagreed with our ideas or the spouse who was unfaithful or left us for someone else. We deal with rejection on two levels—personal and professional; both are equally damaging depending upon how we react.

The Three Stages of Reacting to Rejection

There are three stages of how we react to rejection—I call them the ABCs of dealing with rejection: The **Annoyed Stage,** the **Burdened Stage** and the **Chronic Stage.**

- **Annoyed Stage.** Let's take a personal situation at the annoyed stage. Your friend has a dinner party and she's invited three couples but not you and your spouse. You feel you should have been included. She explains that these three couples share the same interest in outdoor camping and hiking and that she thought you would be bored. Your initial reaction may be a sense of rejection and you may temporarily be miffed. But, in giving it more thought, you admit that an evening talking about camping and hiking would indeed be boring to you and your spouse since you can't stand the sight of bugs and your idea of camping is roughing it at a luxury cabin in the mountains with all the amenities of home. While you may have initially experienced a sense of rejection and it may have been mildly annoying, you accepted your friend's rationale and it did not have a negative impact on the continuation of your friendship.

- **Burdened Stage.** The burdened stage manifests itself more dramatically. Let's use a business situation this time. You feel you have worked hard at your job. All your reviews have been quite good and you are often complimented for being an effective producer. Suddenly your company merges with another industry leader. New ownership takes over and sends in its team. Suddenly you no longer have the same authority; new team members are delegating tasks to you and things have really changed.

While you may not consciously admit to feeling rejected, your distraught feelings indicate that you do feel rejected. At this stage you are inclined to react by resisting change. Whether you express it or not, you are likely beginning to feel that you don't matter to the company any more which is likely to result in your being less enthusiastic, less productive and possibly being angry enough to begin looking for a new job. At this stage you are vulnerable to sabotaging yourself.

- **Critical Stage.** The critical stage is the most damaging. People who respond at this level are often job hoppers (no company ever appreciates them)—they have difficulty in personal relationships (no one ever fully understands them)—and they have lots of excuses for why they are not happy or fulfilled; generally it is someone else's fault.

It has been said that when someone rejects you, it says more about them than it does you. I like what Eleanor Roosevelt said: "People can say 'no' to us millions of times, but no one can reject us unless we reject ourselves."

Here are some guidelines for evaluating rejections and accepting what is without taking it personally:

1. Feel the initial emotion (pain, hurt, anger, etc.); then take time to evaluate why you have responded with this emotion.

2. Determine what specifically triggered the emotion by asking yourself if the specific incident was the main trigger or was it the "break incident" that followed several previous disappointments.

3. Once you have identified the main trigger, attach the emotion to an early life experience in which you felt the same emotion.

4. Once you have identified a basis for the emotional reaction, temporarily prepare yourself to set the emotion aside.

5. Detach your emotions temporarily and consider the event from a strictly logical, factual perspective.

6. In as honest a manner as you can, discuss the situation from a purely factual standpoint with someone you trust who is not emotionally involved. Talking the incident through with another individual brings a fresh perspective to it. For some individuals, writing the facts down first, helps this process.

7. Be open to hearing another point of view.

8. Review the outcome of both the emotional and logical and make your final decision. More than likely, while there may have been some intent on the perpetrator to inflict some emotional pain you will most likely find that the action was not truly a personal rejection.

When you take time to review rejections from this perspective you will often find that it is easier to accept what is (the facts) without taking it personally (emotional attachment). The more you begin to use this process, the more you will be able to balance the power you give to external conditions with the power you give to internal feelings, beliefs and knowledge. Now you are ready for Price Points of Action two, three and four which deal with forgiveness, learning and opportunities.

CHAPTER 3

The Power of Forgiveness

He that cannot forgive others breaks the bridge over which he must pass himself; for every man has need to be forgiven.

—Thomas Fuller

Price Point of Action 2

Acknowledge the Power of Forgiveness at Work, at Home and within Yourself

In order to build mutual trust there must be forgiveness. Therefore, forgiveness is as important in the work force as it is in our personal lives. Just as it takes time to build trust, forgiveness, too, requires time. The deeper the hurt, the longer the process. Minor hurts can be forgiven more quickly. Regardless of the time involved, I believe one thing very strongly. The longer we continue to hang on to the hurt and fail to forgive, the more we actually prevent ourselves from taking control of our lives.

Forgiveness for me was the most difficult process in taking control of my life. I found that while several books had been written on the topic of forgiveness, the process itself was harder to find. Perhaps because forgiving another, even ourselves, happens over a period of time, it has not been easy to chronicle the steps in the process. What I have attempted to do at the end of this chapter therefore, is to recreate the process that I personally went through to deal with my deepest hurt. Use it as a guide. Accept what fits with your values knowing that I share a process that emerged from my values.

My value system says that to forgive does not necessarily mean to forget. It is not the past that needs to be erased, it is the pain that needs to be left behind. The facts are still the facts and the consequences don't change. It is not necessary to forget that your boss lied to you about your future with the company or that a trusted co-worker sabotaged you or took credit for your ideas. It is not necessary to forget that a parent neglected or failed you or that a friend or partner in some way betrayed you. Anger may even be justified. Yet I do believe that the more we practice forgiveness, the more the energy from the anger will become redirected and that the memory of the incident that caused the hurt will reshape itself in our mind, allowing us to experience new learning and understanding and an ability to diminish the pain so that we may move positively forward in our life.

To demonstrate each area of forgiveness, I would like to share examples of professional, personal and self forgiveness. I begin with my earliest recollection of a work incident that needed forgiveness.

A Colleague's Betrayal

Sometimes people hurt us not because they intentionally set out to hurt us, but because they have so little control of their own lives that they act from insecurity, fear or envy.

Early in my career I taught personal development and speech at an east coast junior college of business. Jean, the vice president of admissions, was a stylish, middle-aged woman who traveled throughout the state, making personal development presentations to young high school women about to graduate, in the hope that if they had not yet selected a four-year college, they would select our junior college of business instead. The presentations were a form of recruitment. Jean was great at what she did. But, there was only one of her and, as the year progressed, a heavy schedule created stress that resulted in health problems for her. Nearly every winter she would end up with bronchitis or pneumonia and eventually be sent to bed. In an attempt to alleviate the problem, I was called to the vice president's office one day and asked to consider being a back-up for Jean on days when I did not have heavy classes scheduled. By assigning me to several of the presentation engagements it would lessen Jean's load. I liked the idea. Readily I accepted. The next week I accompanied Jean to several presentations so that I could model mine to be consistent with hers. On one such visit a young teacher mistook me for Jean's daughter, an observation by which Jean was noticeably offended. From that day forward, she treated me with a certain amount of resentment.

Within a few months I was called to the vice president's office again. This time he asked if I could look into the possibility of the college being granted a franchise to conduct a preliminary pageant for the state's Miss America Pageant. My husband and I had been involved in a county pageant that was sponsored by his Jaycees group and I had become quite involved as a chaperon. I knew the state directors quite well, so, I contacted them, requesting that they visit the college to consider giving us a franchise. The school was eventually approved. The directors also recommended that I be very involved because of my experience and knowledge. The school complied. I was later told that Jean and I would be co-executive directors of the pageant, but that she would be involved in name only. I would do the work.

I was young, energetic and willing to please. Although it was a huge job, I recruited other teachers and lots of students and began to plan for a big event. Although we encountered several obstacles, we found creative solutions. For one thing, the administration insisted that we stage the event at a college auditorium rather than a high school because they wanted to enhance the college image. The only facility we could find nearby was Seton Hall University's auditorium which doubled for a gymnasium and had no pull curtain on its stage. Despite being cavernous, we sold enough tickets to fill up the auditorium. As for the lack of a draw-curtain, we dressed all the stage-hands in black and dimmed the lights for a difficult, yet workable resolve to changing sets.

On the night of the pageant the whole hierarchy of the school was there, including the owner who rather begrudgingly agreed to crown the winner. Jean was seated in the front row and merely stood to take a bow as I introduced her as my co-executive director. It was an incredible production; a miniature Miss America Pageant with a musical opening and all the fanfare. At intermission the owner apologized for his earlier attitude, saying that he had no idea what a professional pageant we had put together.

When the event was over the judges had selected a strong, viable state competitor and a wonderful school representative for promotional appearances. At the reception everyone was complimentary; everyone, that is, except Jean. She didn't show up at the reception.

Several weeks later, about two months before the end of the semester, I was summoned to the vice president's office again. With little explanation I was told that my contract would not be renewed. However, he wanted me to fulfill my teaching commitment through the end of the semester as well as to chaperon our representative to the state pageant. Only later did I find out from an admissions representative who worked closely with Jean that she resented the success of the pageant and had demanded that my contract not be renewed. Although it was anything but fair, she had a secret weapon—a personal relationship with the vice president.

I was not yet thirty and very naive about the world of organizational politics, let alone such dirty little things as behind-the-scene affairs, both of which led to my undeserved dismissal. Despite the hurt, I completed the school year, never letting on to the students that I would be leaving. I chaperoned our candidate to the pageant and saw her selected as one of the top ten contenders. When my responsibilities had been completed, I accepted a position from another school for the following year. During that year I learned about forgiveness. Because I was so young, I'm not sure I was aware of the process, yet I truly shifted my thinking and worked to forgive Jean. What is even more amazing to me as I look back on how I handled it, is that when I heard from former colleagues that I was missed, I took the suggestion of one of them and called the President. He asked me to meet with him. During the visit he recalled the events that led up to my departure, explaining that although he did not agree with the decision and its extenuating circumstances, he did feel he needed to back his vice president. He assured me that things would be different if I came back and I assured him that I could put the past behind and work forward. He literally jumped with excitement when he asked, "Then, does this mean you'll accept my offer?" I returned the following semester and continued to work with Jean until two years later when my husband accepted a new job and we moved to Cleveland, Ohio.

Did I forget what Jean had done? No. Remembering the reality of her past actions helped me to know the realities of the situation with which I was working. It also opened the door for me to contribute in my own way and to feel confident as an equal team member. I did forgive her, however, which allowed me to direct my energies toward accomplishing new goals for the organization and it allowed me to perform in a role that I truly enjoyed.

Within work environments there are many reasons that others may treat us unfairly. Sometimes it is dictated by a corporate philosophy or mandated by economic decisions believed to be necessary. Sometimes it happens because another individual's values conflict with our own. Sometimes it's jealousy. Sometimes it's political. Revenge merely escalates the discord and increases the amount of power you give to the wrongdoer. It is a much more powerful experience to forgive the person you believe wronged you.

Forgiveness opens a door for new possibilities and choices; particularly for the one who forgives. When you release the wrongdoer from feelings of resentment and revenge, you free yourself from non-productive, negative energy, allowing you to make more positive choices. Before long you will discover that by forgiving you lessen your burden, heal your memory and regain more control of your life.

Self-Forgiveness

Recently a career outplacement counselor shared with me a wonderful example of self-forgiveness. She related a conversation with a senior executive who had lost his position when his company was reorganized. Unable to find a job of the same magnitude and salary range, he expressed considerable anger, even depression. In particular, he talked of his failure to live up to a commitment he had made to his daughter. He had promised that if she got good grades during the year, he would buy her a car. She had held up her end of the bargain. How could he live with himself if he couldn't live up to his promise?

Emotionally he was beating himself up badly. Although the job loss had been circumstantial, he didn't see how he could forgive himself for not living up to his promise. He was so emotionally caught up in self-punishment that he had totally lost control of his life. The external conditions had overpowered his thinking.

Self-forgiveness takes courage and love. We cannot really forgive ourselves unless we honestly look at whatever it is for which we have condemned ourself. When we cause pain for other people whom we care about and love, the pain becomes inwardly directed toward ourselves. We judge, convict and sentence ourselves. Often we do this secretly. Often the judgment is unjust. Such was the case with this executive.

The fact that the executive expressed his feelings enabled him to begin a self-forgiveness process. Next he was urged to look at what he perceived as a failure with honesty and call it by its right name. This was not his failure. It was an external event that he had little control over which caused him to be in an unemployed state. It may have been uncomfortable, even embarrassing, not to have been able to make good on his promise. But was it a failure? After all, the car was a "thing," an external, non-loving thing. The position that had provided the money for the car was also an external, non-controllable "thing." Yet the love-filled relationship that he had for his daughter was still very much intact. Surely that relationship was of more enduring value than any car could be.

The executive had placed an imbalanced importance on the external (car) and neglected to give equal balance to the internal (love). The fact that his daughter may be disappointed would surely pale in comparison to the loving relationship that could only be strengthened during this time of transition. Years from now, which would be most important—a new car or a father's love?

Forgiving Parental Failures

> *"How many hopes and fears, how many ardent wishes and anxious apprehensions, are twisted together in the threads that connect the parent with the child!"*
>
> —S. G. Goodrich

I strongly relate to the importance of the need for a parent's love. I learned first-hand that money, clothes and "things" do little to make up for the lack of a loving relationship between a parent and child. This is the area from which I had my greatest challenge of forgiveness.

For years each Mother's Day I fought the inner feelings of emptiness and sorrow, so wanting to be like those who embraced the spirit of Mother's Day to celebrate and honor their mothers. Yet I had such mixed feelings about the mother who had chosen not to raise me, leaving me instead to be mothered by an aging grandmother.

When I would question why she had left me I was admonished not to talk about it; it could only hurt my mother I was told. Instead, I was raised to accept my fate and suppress any real feelings of loneliness and need. Perhaps it was the unresolved questions and the years of denying the pain of abandonment that led to my falling apart emotionally in church one Sunday following the minister's traditional Mother's Day sermon.

Oh how I'd wanted my relationship to be the kind he spoke of from the pulpit; one filled with memories of the unconditional love that, "only a mother can give." Intellectually I understood, emotionally I could not relate. With every example of a mother's love he vividly painted, my hurt emotions intensified. At the end of the service when the congregation began to depart, I sat immobilized, trying desperately to hold back the tears that had uncontrollably begun to stream down my face. With shame and embarrassment I eventually departed the church.

Months later I returned. This time to share my secret and to seek some resolve. I remember the stunned expression on the minister's face as I began to relate my background. He seemed even more stunned when I told him about a phone call of a few weeks earlier when my mother had bluntly told me, "I feel I have had to make choices in my life and I simply don't have room for you."

I could understand his shock. For years I had masked my childhood pain well; I looked so normal, whatever that is. I was fairly attractive, well-dressed and carried myself with a self-assured air. My packaging was one of the confidence and success one expects of a child from a loving, supportive home. I had hidden the truth well; sharing the intimate pain with virtually no one in the hopes that one day I could *make* my mother love me. Suddenly, in one phone call, that had all changed. Her words had been so final. Now I needed to let the secret out so I could begin to find a resolve.

Perhaps the most important thing I learned that day is that I was not alone. Unfortunate as it is, not all mothers (or fathers) have behaved in the ways that the minister spoke of from the pulpit that Sunday. Those of us who have experienced a parent's failure, need not deny it, feel guilty or continue to live in pain. Instead, we can learn to forgive and embrace the "Mother Concept;" a wonderful new way of thinking that I learned that day.

The minister pointed out that it is the concept of motherhood and all that it stands for that we honor on this special day. The nurturing, the unconditional love, the belief and caring that depicts mother love. We derive these from many sources beyond birth ties; friends, relatives, teachers, a neighbor who truly cares. These individuals are there if we look for them. But, I had focused so much on what I *didn't* have that I had ignored the wonderful mother love that came from so many others. When I began to change my thinking, I realized how much I had really mattered and how very special I must have been to all those people who had reached out to care so much.

Looking back, I realized that my most vivid "Mother Concepts" had tremendous impact on the fine adult I had become; a strong, loving, intelligent and caring woman who I believed most mothers would be proud to call "daughter."

Among these influencing women was my grandmother. Although stern and sometimes brief and abrupt, I always knew she loved me. It took years of looking back to appreciate how often she protected me by shielding me from small town gossip and family backlash. In other ways she nurtured me by making home baked bread and apple pies, by allowing me to take my furry cat to bed with me each night and by rolling my hair in rags to create long, beautiful curls and then telling me how pretty I was. When I preferred to pretend I was operating my own store or some other make-believe business rather than the traditional girl-thing of playing with dolls, she indulged and encouraged me. In her own way, Grandma instilled in me an entrepreneurial spirit and a sense of confidence.

Mrs. Wilson, my Girl Scout leader was another Mother Concept. She believed in me so strongly that one year, with her urging, I sold more Girl Scout cookies than any other girl scout in Rochester, Minnesota. In a city-wide ceremony she honored me as the Girl Scout Cookie Queen. Now, that may not be a big deal for some people, but for me it was a very proud moment; just one small memory as the result of Mrs. Wilson's constant belief and support.

Mrs. Ellis, the wife of a Mayo Clinic cardiologist, influenced me in another way. I baby sat for the Ellis family during my teen years. Mostly I remember Mrs. Ellis' elegant ways. She was like

Grace Kelly to me; beautiful, polished and always a lady. Unlike others for whom I baby sat, she took time to teach me about the finer things in life. It was from Mrs. Ellis that I acquired a taste for good music and books, learned proper etiquette and a classic sense of style. It was more than exposure; she truly took time to make a difference in my life. I doubt she ever realized the tremendous impact she made.

Noni was my business role model. How I admired her intellect and savvy. During a time when other women were getting married and having babies, Noni chose instead to be married to a career. She imparted to me the importance of dedication and achieving goals. She encouraged me to be professional at whatever career I chose and to always believe in my own abilities, regardless of what obstacles I might encounter.

And, yes, when I allowed myself to be honest, there was even my own mother. Not all memories of her are negative. There were also many good times. They are the ones I've learned to focus on. When I was young, she and my step-father would come to visit. Often they were joyful times filled with fun and laughter. When I got older I was flown to New York city where they lived. I would spend the summer months there and she would take me shopping in New York City, to Broadway musicals and to dine in wonderful restaurants. We'd go to Yankee Stadium to watch Mickey Mantle and Yogi Berra and to swim in the ocean at Jones Beach. In a way, it was living a make-believe life, having marvelous fun with a mother who was only momentarily a part of my life. But there were good times. In retrospect I have learned to be thankful for those good times as I have come to know that for some people, they had few good times.

I have also come to learn that regardless of my abandonment issues, there have always been positive women who have cared about me in motherly ways. Women who fed me emotionally and nurtured me in ways that truly demonstrated mother love. I have come to accept that there are reasons why my own mother could not be there for me in the many ways I needed her. For that I have forgiven her. Yet, in her place were sent some very special women to be my Mother Concepts. Together they have given me a whole new way to think about Mother's Day.

I cannot change the realities of the choices my mother made, yet I can forgive her and in doing so diminish the pain that I hung onto for far too many years. If you have endured pain caused by a parent or loved one, you too can diminish the pain through the process of forgiveness. Here is the process I went through. Perhaps it will be helpful to you:

The Forgiveness Process

1. Identify the specific actions that the individual did to cause you to feel rejected or hurt.

   i.e. Mother caused me to feel the pain of rejection by leaving me with my grandparents instead of keeping me with her.

2. Identify the emotions connected with this action. Be truthful to yourself about the feelings.

   i.e. I felt unworthy, unloved, afraid, alone and insecure.

3. Detach the individual from the hurt and let the hurt go.

   i.e. Letting go is difficult to explain because it is a mental process. For some, a spiritual aspect of letting go is to do all you can do to resolve the situation, then place it in the hands of God (or a higher power). For others, it may be an intellectual process of releasing it from your mind by refusing to dwell upon it.

4. Invite the person back into your mind, void of the emotion, merely acknowledging the facts about what the individual's actions were. Gradually see the deeper truth about the person. The truth is that they hurt us because they are weak, needy, lacking in confidence or have failed to effectively deal with some pain of their own. Edit your memory to see them as they are rather than as powerful enough to hurt you.

   i.e. For whatever reasons, mother was too weak to accept her role. I needed to release her from her wrongdoing and see her as the weak and unhappy individual she was.

5. Viewing the individual with your edited memory, wish them well and feel the powerful emotion of love and healing for them. When you begin to honestly feel that you wish life would go well for them, the forgiveness process has begun.

i.e. Through my edited memory, I began to feel sorry for mother that she had missed so much motherhood joy. Eventually I could honestly wish her the love and joy that I felt toward my own children and wish that she may someday experience the joy of motherhood that I feel as a mother.

6. Be truthful with your feelings to the wrongdoer. State it as fact, own the feelings. Regain your power by establishing limits.

   i.e. I eventually wrote mother a letter expressing my honest feelings about being afraid to ask why she had left me for fear she would leave me forever and how much hurt and pain I had experienced without her love. I concluded the letter with this final paragraph: "Neither you nor I can change all the yesterdays. As much as I have anger and hurt, I do love you in my own special way. And, whether I ever hear from you again or not, that love will not change. But, I will no longer beg for your love in return. That is a decision only you can make."

   This step can be handled face-to-face or with a letter. It may even be that you write the letter, but never mail it. The important aspect is to confront the honest feelings so that you can move forward and live from here-on within new limits.

7. Consciously begin to replace the feelings of hurt with feelings of love.

   i.e. I personally sought help from God through prayer for this, asking that He fill me with the feeling of His love that I may send through prayer those loving emotions to mother.

8. Acknowledge that forgetting is not part of the forgiveness process. You cannot forgive people for things you forget. The important part of forgiveness is that we have the power to forgive what we still remember. Forgiving is not excusing, accepting, tolerating or denying. It is confronting, releasing and setting new boundaries that enable us to start over with someone who has hurt us, should we choose to.

   i.e. I have let go of the pain mother's actions caused, yet I make no excuses for the decisions she made. I know that she was ac-

> *countable for her actions, I do not have to tolerate what she did, nor do I make things better by denying and pretending that it was not as painful as it was. Instead, I accept the realities and in doing so realize that by forgiving I give forth a love that in return frees me to take control of my life instead of allowing past hurts and actions (external conditions) to rob me of that right.*

The power of forgiving helps us to know that past, external situations no longer have control over us. When we forgive fully, the hurt and anger of the past will eventually fade and in its place optimism and strength will begin to flourish, giving us the power to control a new, more positive future.

CHAPTER

4

Learning and Purpose

There are three classes of people in the world. The first learn from their own experience these are wise; the second learn from the experience of others these are happy; the third neither learn from their own experience nor the experience of others these are fools.

—Chesterfield

Price Point of Action 3

Embrace Each Moment for Its Learning and Purpose

There is a danger when we live too long in a comfort zone. Challenges stretch us, often thrusting us into new experiences we may otherwise have been reluctant to choose.

When external conditions such as job loss, position loss, bruised relationships and outright rejection happen to us, it is important at some point to take time to look at the situation with insight and identify what was learned from it. Nearly always there is learning.

A middle-aged executive who was forced to take early retirement several years ago felt resentment at first. As a highly educated engineer he feared that younger engineers with more contemporary training would be stiff competition in his quest to find a new job. After reflecting upon his new situation, he concluded that the retirement had provided an opportunity rather than a dilemma. When he turned inward and thought honestly about his life, he discovered a truth he had long buried. Engineering was actually never something he had been passionate about. He had just gotten good grades in all the necessary subjects, and when all of his high school buddies applied to A & M University for an engineering major, he had gone along with them. He continued to get good grades and naturally gravitated to an engineering position with a major technology company after graduating. Because he was good at what he did, he became successful. But, in reality, he never really loved what he did. What he had always had a love for was painting — western, rustic painting. No money in that though; certainly not enough to support a wife, then family. So, he had taken the engineering path; it provided more stability.

With his family life stable, children married, the last one finishing college, now he could pursue what he loved to do. Today he paints art and sells it. Perhaps it is not as lucrative as his corporate job, yet the sense of accomplishment and fulfillment provide a totally different compensation — one that he treasures at this stage in life.

What this former corporate executive realized is what some people fail to understand. At different stages in our life there are different purposes for us to serve. Giving power to a society view that infers you are no longer successful if you get off the corporate ladder merely creates imbalance and diminishes the ability to control your own life. What is important is being able to objectively recognize what your purpose is at each new stage. This recognition becomes part of the learning process.

Earl's Boxed Thinking Theory

Having just left the CBS television affiliate in Kansas City to join an advertising agency, I got a call one day from Earl Beale. Earl was the General Manager of the NBC affiliated television station. He explained that his weekend weather reporter was moving into a weekend anchor spot and that until he found a permanent replacement, he needed an experienced television talent to do the weekend weather until he hired someone to fill in for the weekday weatherman while he went on vacation. Would I consider taking the position, he asked.

With little hesitation I thanked him for thinking of me but told him I thought I was too old to be a "weather girl." In my mind, all women who did weather at that time were much younger than me and sort of cutesy — not a style that seemed to fit me.

"People put people in boxes," he said, "not the situation. Think it over and call me back."

I learned a lot from him. He was absolutely right. I had narrow vision. He challenged me to widen it. Soon I began to think about how I could gain from the experience; how I could bring my own style to the position; how I might actually enjoy the expedience, let alone the extra money. I called him back, took the position and had an absolutely wonderful time in a temporary job that was a great learning experience that stretched me as an on-camera talent, to say nothing of the on-air exposure which served a valuable purpose. Months later I found that my recognition factor in the community from that television exposure was an instrumental factor in helping me to be selected for the Society Editor position at *The Kansas City Star.*

How boxed is your thinking? When unplanned external situations challenge you, do you see the learning possibilities or merely the challenge?

When we embrace each moment for its learning and purpose we are better able to balance our thinking, thus take more control of our own lives.

CHAPTER 5

Recognizing Opportunities

When one door of happiness closes, another opens; but often we look so long at the closed door that we do not see the one which has been opened for us.

—Helen Keller

▼ Price Point of Action 4

Open Yourself to Opportunities; Look for the Potential

In times of adversity we often relinquish power to the external situation rather than view it as an opportunity. Just as it is important to embrace each moment for its learning and purpose, it is equally important to look for new opportunities in situations disguised as problems. This takes objectivity, even creativity.

When my husband accepted a job in Cleveland, Ohio, I was forced to give up a career which had taken four years to build. I was uncertain as to what I would do after the move. Concerned, I sought suggestions from colleagues. One was a man from McGraw-Hill who had hired me to conduct teacher training seminars to implement a McGraw-Hill text book. His advice surprised me.

"I think you should go into television," he suggested, explaining that he thought I had a knack for drawing people out and would be a good interviewer. Plus, I used a video camera in the classroom for speech and visual poise training. I liked the idea, but I had absolutely no television background, let alone training.

However, the more I thought about it, the more I began to see it as a possible opportunity.

Making Things Happen

Upon arriving in Cleveland, I began to call television stations. I was so green I didn't even know who to ask for or quite how to answer questions about what exactly I wanted to do. But I was persistent and, in the meantime, I began to volunteer for organizations such as the Downtown Restoration Society, the Women's Committee of the Great Lakes Shakespeare Festival and Women's City Club. The more I began to know about the community, the more I began to see how there were wonderful stories to be told. So, I continued to call the television stations. Eventually I began to break some barriers. In retrospect, the first station probably gave me an audition to get me to stop calling. Nevertheless, I got my first opportunity to read news from an anchor desk. Although they didn't hire me, it was one more step in the learning process.

Next came an interview with a man named Ernie Sindelar. He was the program director for the ABC television affiliate. Something I said on the phone intrigued him and he gave me an interview. At the end of the session he informed me that if I had called just one week earlier he would have most likely hired me for a co-host position on their early morning talk show. Disappointed, I asked him why he had me come in when he knew the position was gone. "Because I thought from our conversation you might have potential," he said. "And, you do." He became my mentor. He set up an audition, reviewed the tape with me, coached me on what worked and what didn't and encouraged me to keep pursuing my dream. He fostered a belief that I did have what it took to break into this top ten television market despite my lack of experience. He also taught me an important lesson.

Nothing is new in this business, he told me. It's what *you* bring to it.

Several months later I was hired by the NBC owned and operated station as a contributing editor for a once-a-week news and information show. A few months later I was named co-hostess of the show, and a mini-documentary which I co-produced with my producer was nominated for a local Emmy Award. It took me exactly one year to break into television. But, with perseverance, belief and commitment I was open to every possible opportunity. And I never forgot Ernie Sindelar's words of wisdom and valued what I brought to the possibilities.

What opportunities have you failed to see as opportunities? Could it be that in taking a temporary step backward, you might find a new path to an even greater opportunity? Even chieftains have to take a step backward sometimes. I remember Howard Putnam, former CEO of Braniff Airlines, talking to a speaker's association meeting several years ago. When asked how he handled it when Braniff failed, he replied that sometimes you have to step backward to step forward again.

Create Opportunities

Another option is to create your own opportunities. When the external forces shake you up and out, take control by creating something new for yourself. Today small business is the driving economic force of our nation. Most small business are actually what I call mini-businesses, ones with less than five employees. According to *The State of Small Business: A Report of the President*, 90 percent of the new jobs from 1989 to 1991 came from companies with four or less employees. *The 1992 U. S. Census Bureau Report on Small Business* reports that of the more than 19 million small businesses, 17 million are sole proprietorships, partnerships or subchapter S corporations. Thirty-three percent are women-owned. Women, more than any other group of business people, have emerged strong from corporate downsizing and upward mobility barriers. Rather than be overcome by external events, they have taken control by creating and succeeding at building their own businesses. It's the American dream, it's an option for you and you don't need a fortune to start one. You do, however, need to think out of the comfort box.

For the past seven years I have taught a course at a Community College on How to Start Your Own Consulting Business. The most important part of the entire ten-hour class seems to be the module developed to jog the thinking. I remember when merged out executives from middle management to vice presidents started popping up in the class. When they described their experience prior to "transition," I felt so inferior. How could I possibly teach these people anything about business, I thought momentarily. Yet I found that I could, and the greatest gift was helping them to see options outside of the corporate box. To this day I find it exhilarating to see someone's light bulb go off when they realize they have opportunities to use their talents, experience and skills in new and challenging ways. And, it's exciting for them when they discover the wisdom of Ernie Sindelar and realize that what they bring to new opportunities is their own unique selves.

If you're stuck in a rut, allowing the external pressures to imbalance your thinking, think again. Get out and talk to people who are already doing something that sounds interesting to you. Read every book you can get your hands on about opportunities and possibilities. Read success stories about others and see how their process might relate to you. Read *Home Office Computing* and *Entrepreneur Magazine*; they're filled with business ideas and successes large and small.

Begin looking at the world with a new set of eyes. When shopping, look for what's missing and think about how you can fill the void. When talking with people find out what product or service they can never find or find a shortage of, then think how you can fill the need. Listen between the lines. Get into people, instead of yourself. Volunteer, get involved and become an innocent, inquisitive child again.

Life is full of opportunities. Sometimes we fail to look below the surface. Open up the box, shake it around, have fun. Who knows, you just might discover a whole new way to bring joy and happiness back into your life.

CHAPTER 6

Who Are You?

Everything without tells the individual he
is nothing; everything within persuades him
that he is everything.

—Xavier Douddan

PRINCIPLE #2

Know and Value the Difference Between "Who" You Are and "What" You Are and Know That You Matter

When our thinking about ourself is imbalanced, we are not consistent with our true self. As a result, we tend to take rejections personally and allow external actions, situations and events to dominate our thinking, discounting the power we actually have to take control of our lives. When our thinking is balanced, we know the difference and our life and actions reflect it.

Take the case of former Dallas Cowboys Super Bowl star, James Washington.

A friend of mine who was doing some promotional work with James, called me one day to discuss James' interest in possibly doing some motivational speaking. Because of my background, she thought it would be helpful for me to talk with him. We met for dinner. As we talked, James related a childhood of growing up in the Watts section of Los Angeles, surrounded by uncertainty, crime and death. By the time he had reached senior high school, several of the friends he had grown up with had become death statistics either violently or from drugs. I wondered what had been different about James.

He attributed his path to an inner strength, a foundation that had been laid by a loving and wise grandmother and reinforced by a caring teacher. He told me that whenever he would feel himself being drawn out of control by the things going on around him, he followed the advice of a teacher from a very early grade. She told James that he could go into his own room and quietly picture himself being successful at whatever he wanted for himself.

Because his grandmother's home was modest and James didn't have a room of his own, he questioned how he might follow the teacher's suggestion. With wonderful wisdom, his grandmother found a solution. She gave James a ball of string and suggested that whenever he needed to be alone with his thoughts, to use the string to create a small room and to pretend that he was sitting in there privately.

What a wonderful legacy James' grandmother left for him, a legacy that no money could surpass, the ability to fully use the power of his mind.

As Xavier Douddan's quote denotes, everything without (external) demonstrated that James' life was destined for failure, possibly even death, for negativity surrounded him. Yet everything within (internal) persuades him that he is everything, that he can use the power of his mind to take control of his life, remove himself from his disadvantaged situation and become successful and positive.

James was a young impoverished man, yet he was bright, visionary and internally strong. I believe James is a sterling example of someone who knew the difference between "who" he was and "what" he was. And certainly, through the unconditional love imparted to him by his grandmother during his young, formative years, he knew and believe that he mattered. How about you?

Through my own research, I have found that often our life gets so imbalanced with the external aspects that we lose sight of who we really are. This is particularly evident for the thousands of individuals who are forced to deal with transition due to today's economically turbulent business climate. I can relate because I have experienced it myself.

Only through reestablishing self-worth and redefining yourself, will you be able to balance "who" and "what" you are in a way that will enable you to move forward to gain new personal and professional fulfillment.

The following Price Point Action Steps will help you to make Principle #2 work for you:

- ▼ Be yourself
- ▼ X-Out past failures
- ▼ Reject rejection
- ▼ Invest in yourself

CHAPTER 7

Who Do You Think You Are?

*When one is a stranger to oneself, then
one is estranged from others, too.*
—Anne Morrow Lindbergh

▼ Price Point of Action 5
Be Yourself

Who are you?

While this may sound like a simple question, your answer will serve as a starting point for you to take an honest look at just how well you actually know yourself. It will begin to provide understanding for how you may react to rejections and disappointments in your life and to how well you are able to cope with uncertainty and take control of your life in uncontrollable times.

In the space provided below, write down as many words or phrases as you can to describe who you think you are. There are no right or wrong answers. There are no magical numbers. You may make a long or short list, although a minimum of five is suggested; your list may contain many single words or it may be made up of several descriptive phrases. There is no significance to the order in which you list things, simply write quickly and without labored thought as descriptions come to your mind. Time is a factor. It is best to take no more than five minutes to complete this exercise. How you choose to describe who you are is less important than getting your thoughts down in black and white so you can refer to them later. When your list is complete, continue reading:

Who are you? I am.....

______________________ ______________________

______________________ ______________________

______________________ ______________________

______________________ ______________________

______________________ ______________________

______________________ ______________________

Debbie participated in a group workshop and here are the descriptions she listed in response to the question, "Who am I?" She wrote, I am....

- Wonderful
- Happy
- Content
- Fortunate to have a good job
- Giving
- Busy
- Stressed
- Friendly
- 40 years old
- Five foot seven
- A wife
- A Christian believer
- Hurting
- Blessed with a loving family
- Patient
- Opinionated
- Behind in my work
- Searching
- Warm
- A secretary
- Married
- A mother

- Special in God's eyes
- An American
- Privileged to be born in the USA
- A perfectionist

Another member of the group, George, wrote, I am....:

- A manager
- Capable making good decisions
- A good provider
- A father
- Bright
- A leader
- A member of the team
- Well-paid
- A husband
- Good at stock market investing
- An athlete
- A community volunteer

Some of the words and phrases used by Debbie and George relate to "who" they are. Other words relate more to "what" they are. Let's take Debbie's list, for example. She used emotional and behavioral traits such as, "giving, friendly, blessed with a loving family, opinionated, content, happy, hurting, searching." These elements make her the unique individual she thinks about as herself. They are behaviors or values that make up "who" she is. Debbie also listed several words such as, "secretary, American, Christian, wife and mother;" each of which denote a person, a comparison, a thing or an externally judged quality, and relate more to "what" she is. The fact that Debbie listed feelings such as hurting and searching, simply indicate her willingness to acknowledge that some of her true self is made up of characteristics she is consciously dealing with.

Overall, Debbie's list is quite balanced with "who" and "what." As a result, Debbie will be less likely to view rejections that she encounters as personal. Her strong sense of self will help her to realize that not every rejection she encounters has something to do with her as a person. She will be balanced enough in her thinking that even though she might not understand the specific reason when uncertainty or rejection comes into her life, she will be able to detach herself personally from it and employ coping skills that will help her to take control of her life.

George, on the other hand, has a less balanced list. Nearly everything on his list deals with "what" he is: "a provider, a father, a manager, a leader." As a result, when George encounters rejection or uncertainty that relates to his life, he will be very likely to take it personally. He is more tied to "what" he is than "who" he is.

As Society Editor at *The Kansas City Star*, I frequently saw this imbalance in individuals. Frequently I saw this in high-ranking executives, even more often in their spouses. The results were always apparent, sometimes devastating. One woman whose husband had been in a senior vice president role felt so rejected by her country club friends when her husband lost his job, that she simply could not cope with her new role. Her inability to redefine herself cost her more than popularity at the country club or position in the community. It cost her the ability to function as an individual. She felt so connected to being "Mrs. Vice President," that when her husband's role changed, she felt embarrassed, less important, suddenly no one. Her inability to cope eventually resulted in a severely strained marriage, which in turn eroded her self-image even more. One year after her husband lost his position, she admitted herself to a clinic, and considered shock therapy.

While this woman may be an extreme example, she does represent the dramatic impact that can occur from an inability to deal with rejection and external factors which we are forced to deal with from time to time.

Your Self-View

Your Self-View — how you see yourself — is made up of three areas: **Self-Esteem, Role Awareness** and **Self-Direction.**

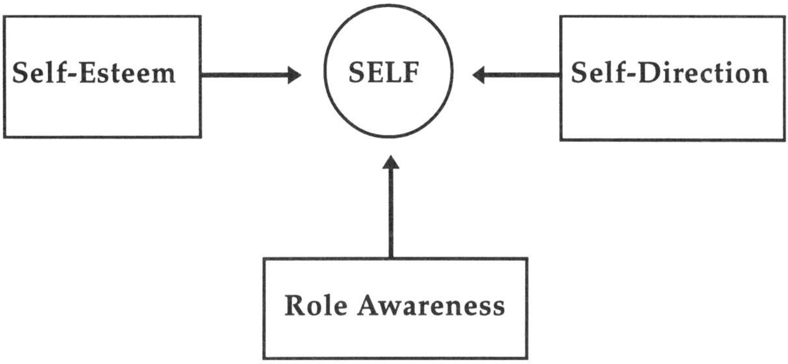

To deal with rejection effectively and take control of your life, it is important to understand each area and to strive to give each a realistic importance. When too much emphasis is placed on self-esteem, you may be overly sensitive and tend to personalize all forms of rejection. If you place too much emphasis on role awareness, you will be even more likely to take rejections personally because of the lack of value you place on your unique inner qualities. If you are overly self-directed you will also have a tendency to take rejections personally or allow external situations to control your life because of your obsession with self-imposed rules, such as how you *should* act and how you *ought* to perform.

Your Self-Esteem

Your self-esteem provides your own measurement of how you value yourself as a unique person. It is simply your ability to see and understand who you are, set apart from what anyone else thinks about you or from what you expect from yourself. It denotes your own perception of self-importance and enables you to say, "I am valuable and special just for who I am." This is your essence of being, your lovability as a person with a unique personality presence and spiritual worth.

Your Role Awareness

Your role awareness measures how you value your present social and/or role situations, your role as a mother, father, wife or teacher, secretary, executive, etc. It indicates your self-measurement of how you perceive yourself to be functioning in your roles or socially. This reveals your ability to feel comfortable and confident about the role you are serving, including how clearly you understand the requirements of your social and role situations. How much of a practical commodity are you right now? What comparative value do you have and how do you compare with others in your social setting, your profession, your age group, among your peers?

Your Self-Direction

Your self-direction reveals how you believe you *should* be and what you believe you *ought* to do. It indicates what you are driven to achieve based on the ideas you have of how you think you should behave, what you should stand for. It is revealed by situations such as whether you need to be number one or can you feel satisfied knowing that being third or fourth you have still performed well given your experience, knowledge or talent. A good example would be pitting yourself against a high-ranking tennis player when you are at an intermediate stage. Even though you may not win the game, if you feel you played well, you would have felt good about playing so well in that particular situation.

Balancing All Three

Self-Esteem

When your **self-esteem** is in balance, you will think optimistically and positively about yourself and who you are as a unique individual, your feelings and your personality. When you are overly attentive to this part of yourself, you will engage in self-pity and doubt, fearing that others will not give you enough credit or value you highly enough. Overemphasis in self-esteem causes you to take rejection personally and causes you to feel that you are personally not appreciated, liked or valued.

When you discount your unique value, you will have a tendency to pay too much attention to your character flaws or too little attention to your character strengths. By not giving yourself the benefit of doubt, you will feel skeptical about your unique self-value and will be vulnerable to external actions and situations.

Role Awareness and Self-Direction

When your **role awareness** and **self-direction** is in balance, you will understand the value of comparing yourself to others and perform your role with confidence. When you are over-attentive to this part of yourself, you will feel excessively conscious of your social/role image and will tend to expect too much from your position or role. You will be easily disappointed because you expect more out of your role or position than can be realized, thus making yourself vulnerable to perceived rejections or actions for which you cannot possibly control.

Decision-Making

When you discount your **role awareness** or **self-direction** it generally indicates that you are frustrated or indecisive about whether your present role or status allows you to maximize your potential. You will feel uncomfortable being compared to others and you will feel that you are not able to function as fully as you think you are capable of in your present situation (role or social). Again, this makes you vulnerable to personalizing rejection and uncontrollable external conditions.

While there is no perfect balance, the important thing is to be aware of all three areas of your self. Where there is imbalance, strive to bring your thinking in that area more into balance.

Since your self-image is the standard from which you make decisions, when your self-image is accurate—close to being how you truly are—you are able to make consistent choices that result in personal success, joy, growth, adaptability and overall better relationships with others. You are able to make decisions that provide personal fulfillment rather than merely satisfying other's expectations. You will be able to recognize rejection and external factors in a more objective and realistic manner, and thus take greater control of your life in uncontrollable times.

When your self-image is not consistent with how you really are, you limit your ability to make accurate judgments which, in turn, increases frustration and stress and leads to making invalid and biased decisions. In essence, it becomes a form of self-deception. In the words of Plato, "The worst of all deceptions is self-deception."

An Accurate Self-Image

An example of an accurate self-image is a 40-year-old woman who has been an accountant. She becomes tremendously interested in the field of medicine but realizes she does not have the current educational background to realistically change career fields. She decides to take a job in a related field while she re-educates herself at a nearby college taking evening courses in medical technology.

The Self That Distorts Skills

An example of an inaccurate self-image is a 40-year-old man who decides that because he's been quite successful selling office equipment he can achieve more independence and make more money selling real estate. Although he fails the real estate course two times in a row, he continues to relate to people based on his self-image as a future big-time player in the real estate industry. He will exert himself in ways that ultimately will prove frustrating and futile. When people who have different perceptions about him hold opinions that vary from his beliefs, he will react to comments and advice negatively. From his perspective, their advice will be stupid, biased and unwelcome. Eventually, he will feel rejected by anyone who disagrees with him and the vision he has built of himself. The friends he will have will become those who care enough about him to either not tell him the truth (believing that he would not be able to handle it at this point) or those who actually agree with his distorted self-assessment.

The Self That Prevents Listening

Remember Kevin, the salesman you read about earlier who insisted that he had been rejected personally? Kevin places a high emphasis on people liking him and/or building strong relationships. He believes that he can best create sales by building relationships, thus he relies tremendously on the self-esteem area. While building relationships may be a valid strategy to long-term sales results, Kevin places the highest value on his ability to build relationships and see others as unique individuals. He discounts practical issues. He is overly attentive to being empathic and has pre-set ideas about what *should* and *ought* to happen when he places all his emphasis on pleasing the customer. Because his perceptions are so imbalanced, he has a blind spot when it comes to hearing anything practical or contrary to his own belief system.

You will recall that Kevin said he had several conversations with the prospect prior to a face-to-face visit. In Kevin's mind, he believed he was building an important relationship. In his mind, that was the only thing that counted. So, when the prospect agreed to meet with Kevin, he thought he was calling on someone with whom he had established a basic relationship. With Kevin's mind set, any practical information offered by the prospect (like, I already have most of my equipment), would have been given little value by Kevin. He simply would not have heard the veiled comments of disinterest, regardless of how many hints may have been given. Instead, unless Kevin heard a firm "no," he would have persisted in his efforts to gain from the relationship.

Once Kevin persisted to the point of setting up a face-to-face meeting (which simply could have been that the prospect gave in to Kevin's persistence, thinking he would get rid of him by agreeing to meet with him once), Kevin entered the meeting with a mind set that said, "I have built a relationship with you, you like me and you are ready to move forward and do business with me." Instead, when the prospect expressed not caring for the company or the product and asked Kevin to leave, Kevin felt personally rejected. Because emotional and "should-based" thinking dominated Kevin's actions, he allowed external conditions to take control and continued to hang on to the feelings of rejection.

Because of Kevin's imbalanced thinking, his self-image is not consistent with his true self.

How Are You Connected?

Today, psychologists are finding that too many people connect more to "what" they are than "who" they are, placing more value on things like job, title, salary, or position in the community, than their unique personality, lovability and presence. At the beginning of this chapter you wrote down words and phrases to describe who you are. Turn back to this list and look at it. Have you written words like mother, father, manager, entrepreneur, leader, lawyer, successful, well-respected, important? Or have you written more words like confident, capable, loving, persistent, friendly, competent, organized, understanding, a caring human being? Have you included any negative descriptions like frustrated, always late, possessive, short-tempered?

You will want to achieve a balance in your list. Review the list for those descriptions which depict external aspects of your life, such as "parent, manager, doctor, secretary." These reflect your **role awareness.** Then check for the number of words such as "loving, caring, organized, competent, confident." These represent characteristics that make you uniquely you. They reflect your **self-esteem**. Finally check for words, such as "behind schedule, frustrated, first place, among the top achievers." These represent your **self-direction**. They reflect how you compare your actions against how you believe you *ought* or *should* perform.

Your **self-esteem** list connects you to "**who**" you are; your **role awareness** and **self-direction** list ties more to "**what**" you are.

If your list shows that you feel more connected with "what" you are than "who" you are, you will want to become more aware of the importance you place on your role awareness and self-direction. Being imbalanced in these areas will make you more vulnerable to external events and actions for which you will have little control over. If your list is imbalanced with too many wonderful characteristics of "who" you are, you will also want to take note to become more aware that the image you hold of yourself is accurate.

It has been said that a strength overused becomes a weakness. When your thinking about yourself is more equally balanced in the three dimensions, you will find that your strengths will work more effectively for you, help you to reflect a stronger image of your true self and, in being your true self, make you better able to take control of your life in uncontrollable times.

CHAPTER 8

Miss Wenstrom

Failure is often God's own tool for carving some of the finest outlines in the character of his children; and, even in this life, bitter and crushing failures have often in them the germs of new and quite unimagined happiness.

—Thomas Hodgkin

Price Point of Action 6

X-Out Past Failures

It's interesting how we view failures. Sometimes we think we've failed ourselves; other times we anguish, thinking we have failed others. Sometimes our failures seem little to us; other times failure overwhelms us. The way we view failure and cope with failures can dramatically shape our future.

As I write the final chapters of this book, I can't help but think about the suicide of Admiral Jeremy Boorda, chief of naval operations, who shot himself prior to a scheduled meeting with *Newsweek* magazine reporters to discuss allegations that he was not entitled to wear "V" — for valor — pins on two medals he was awarded for service in the Vietnam War.

Retired 4-star admiral Elmo R. Zumwalt Jr., a Vietnam era chief of naval operations, when interviewed in both the print and broadcast media about the tragedy said Adm. Boorda, as the Navy's top admiral, coped with tremendous responsibilities and pressures, and then he was suddenly faced 'with the prospect that these guys are going to come in and make him look like he'd done something wrong. I can see how it could suddenly become overwhelming,' he said."[1]

News reports confirmed that a one-page suicide letter written by Adm. Boorda, "poured out his fear that a dispute over the legitimacy of two of his wartime medals would harm the battered reputation of the Navy."[2]

Clearly the possible humiliation of the admiral and the questioning of his integrity played major roles in the suicide. Yet one has to question the imbalance of power he chose to give to the external conditions (Principle #1) and the imbalance of his ability to know and value the difference between "who" he was, and "what" he was (Principle #2). Instead of facing the adversity head-on and dealing with the consequences, the admiral made a tragic choice.

Certainly Admiral Boorda's situation reflects an extreme. Yet, having spent a portion of my career as a development director for a major suicide and crisis center, I know first-hand that this alternative is considered far more often than one might think. And, all too frequently, it is men who believe they have failed in their careers who make this choice. According to Diane Stafford, a reporter for *The Kansas City Star*, "More and more successful professional men in their 30s and 40s are suffering depression." In her article *For more baby boomers, life's highway takes a detour through the men's gloom*, she quotes Ronald Kessler, sociology professor at the University of Michigan's Institute for Social Research, as saying that "the 1990s rate of depression is rising significantly faster among men than among women."[3]

"Even the smallest failure can prove crushing to an ego that's fragile," says clinical psychologist Marvin Aronson, senior supervisor at the Postgraduate Center for Mental Health in New York. "A lot of successful people can have a number of little failures that really wound them deeply. To an outsider this often seems puzzling."[4]

---

[1]Dallas Morning News, Saturday, May 18, 1996
[2]Dallas Morning News, Saturday, May 18, 1996
[3]New York Times News Service, March, 1996, *For more baby boomers, life's highway takes a detour through the men's gloom*, Diane Stafford, Kansas City Star
[4]Dallas Morning News, Thursday, February 21, 1991

Perhaps it is time to rethink what failure is.

English poet John Keats wrote, "Failure is, in a sense, the highway to success, inasmuch as every discovery of what is false leads us to seek earnestly after what is true, and every fresh experience points out some form of error which we shall afterward carefully avoid." Not everyone looks at failure so philosophically, however.

Failure Traps

Today, there are many pressures disguised as failure traps. Companies pressure employees to outperform and overextend in a scaled back work force. The pressure of dealing with child care issues has been compounded with elder care issues. As more women succeed in corporate America and at running their own businesses, men are replaced by their wives as primary breadwinners. If one perceives that they are ill equipped to cope with all this stress, they may see themselves as failures. Thus, it is more important than ever to re-evaluate your thinking and give your values priority.

When I think about x-ing out past failures, I always think back to an early incident when I thought I had failed. It's a perfect example of how I allowed someone else's values to determine whether I would be a success or a failure.

Miss Wenstrom

During the era that I grew up, women's major career choices were to be a teacher, a nurse or an executive secretary. I had been urged to pursue the latter. My role model was Perry Mason's secretary, Della Street, from the popular mystery television show. I dreamed of working for a top executive in New York City after graduating from high school, so I took classes in typing and shorthand, skills required at that time. Typing class went very well; I tested well over 100 words per minute. Somehow the skill came naturally. Shorthand, however, was another story. Miss Wenstrom was my shorthand teacher and her minimum standards required that I take shorthand at 120 words per minute, a feat I could never quite accomplish.

Miss Wenstrom had a commanding presence. She stood about five foot ten, was large boned and walked firmly with a confident stride. She always wore tailored, expensive-looking suits, flowery perfume and very little jewelry. She wore just enough makeup to embellish the natural blush on her high-boned cheeks and to complete the arch of her stern, peaked brows. Her long grey hair was piled neatly on top of her head and monthly she enhanced the grey by dying it with blueing.

I was not a favorite student of Miss Wenstrom because I couldn't seem to get past 80 words per minute in shorthand. It should have been no surprise that when I was called to Miss Wenstrom's office for a personal conference before graduation, her predictions for my future were not the brightest. However, I hardly expected the dismal message she delivered.

"Bette, you will never be a secretary," she said matter-of-factly. And to prove it, she gave me a "D" for my final grade. To me, it was an "F." I had certainly failed. My skills were tarnished; I didn't make the grade. My dreams were shattered and I believed Miss Wenstrom.

After graduation I went to New York as planned. There I met a young man who was a chemical engineer for Union Carbide. He suggested I apply for a job there. Dressed like Della Street, I headed for 42nd Street in New York City to the personnel offices of this giant corporation and applied for a clerk typist position. After all, I wasn't qualified to be a secretary and I certainly couldn't risk failing the shorthand test. I was hired and placed in the district sales office for the Chemicals Division. There I did a fine job at a variety of somewhat unchallenging tasks. Then one day the sales manager's secretary was out sick and he needed someone to take dictation. He was desperate. "Doesn't anyone else in this office know shorthand?" he asked with frustration. Rather sheepishly I replied, "I do. But I can't take it too fast." Since no one else volunteered, he called me into his office and began to dictate.

I learned the most amazing thing that day—not everyone speaks at 120 words a minute. Not only did I get all the dictation, I completed the task in a timely and quality manner. Soon, I was being asked to take dictation by others in the office and eventually I began to rethink my concept of failure.

One block away from my office was the Airline Building. I had always been fascinated with the airlines and I began to think, if I could actually take shorthand, maybe I could get hired as a secretary in the airline industry. One day during lunch hour I decided to give it a try. The position I applied for was secretary/

receptionist at National Airlines. Mr. Reid, the personnel director, called me to his office after I had completed all the tests. Guess what test I had failed. The shorthand test. "I'm going to hire you anyway," he said, confiding that my all-around skills compensated for my low score on shorthand. I was thrilled. Two weeks later I began my new job. Within a few months the personnel director's secretary left and I replaced her. By the end of the year the vice president's secretary decided to leave and he asked for me. Wow! There I was—less than two years out of high school, working in New York City as the executive secretary for the vice president of one of the largest airlines—and, I wrote Miss Wenstrom a letter.

Miss Wenstrom never wrote back. It didn't matter. What mattered was that I realized very early in my career that other people's values do not dictate my success or failure. Least we get too filled with our own self-importance or believe that perfection is achievable, failures will be a part of our life's journey. It is how we learn and grow from the failures that strengthen our wisdom during the journey.

What failure have you not yet x'd out? Are you being too influenced by someone else's thinking? Whose agenda are you living by? Take this quiz for some additional insight:

By Whose Agenda Are You Living?

In the following quiz, give yourself 4 points for each **always** answer, 3 points for **usually**, 2 for **seldom** and 1 for **never.**

______ 1. When you and your friends go out to a movie, do you choose the movie?

______ 2. If you wanted to spend your vacation at the beach and your spouse wanted to go to the mountains, would you wind up going to the beach?

______ 3. If you tried on a suit and liked it very much but your best friend thought it was inappropriate for you, would you buy it?

______ 4. If you wanted Mexican food for dinner and your date/spouse wanted to eat Chinese instead, would you comment on your preference?

______ 5. If you were asked to serve on the board of directors for a non-profit organization, but you were on three other boards and didn't feel you could handle another one, would you explain your feelings and ask to be excused from the new board?

______ 6. In a restaurant, if you ordered your steak well-done and it was brought to you rare, would you send it back?

______ 7. A client invites you to a multi-level marketing meeting and you have absolutely no interest in this type of business, would you politely turn down the invitation and explain your position?

______ 8. A co-worker is always slacking off, creating a heavier work load on you. Would you confront the co-worker about this behavior?

______ 9. A lateral position is offered to you within the company but you have your eye on a position that you think may become available soon. Your boss says your taking this position will greatly help improve communication between the two departments. Will you accept the offer?

______ 10. You have tickets for a baseball game that you've been excited about attending. Your boss calls you in that morning and tells you he wants you to go to a charity dinner in his place because he's been to one too many galas this month. Will you go in his place?

Here's how to score yourself:

40 points — You have a really strong self-image. You live your life by no one's agenda but your own. People probably have some strong impressions about you.

30 - 39 — You don't seem to have many problems either. You seem to balance your own desires with con-

cern about other people's feelings, yet you are not afraid to stick up for what you want.

25 - 29 It is not easy for you to stand up for what you want. More often than not, you find yourself living by the other person's rules.

13 - 19 You might want to think about making some serious changes in your approach to life. Your needs are not being met often enough. You will be more balanced and in control if you learn to express your needs more often.

11 - 12 Please don't eat the pages of this book. You do make a few decisions for yourself, but extreme changes are needed if you are going to have more control of your life.

10 HELP! HELP!

CHAPTER 9 The Cycle of Rejection

"Life can only be understood backwards,
but it must be lived forwards."
—Soren Kierkegaard

▼ Price Point of Action 7
Reject Rejection

Where do feelings of rejection begin? They actually begin the day we are born.

Your adult behavior stems from beliefs established at an early age. Psychologists tell us that the period from birth to age seven constitutes the most formidable years, those when you establish a basic belief system. Regardless of race, religion, ethnic heritage or economic background, we all begin life with one primary purpose: **to matter.**

When the verbal and physical messages you receive during these early years convey unconditional love, you establish feelings that you are important and have value — you matter. When the messages are negative, disparaging or critical, you begin to develop feelings of being less important. Three primary elements work to establish your base feelings: 1) Your parents or primary care-givers, 2) Specific events, and 3) your personal environment. One, or any combination of these elements, can set the stage for your feelings of acceptance or rejection. When the dominant feeling is rejection, it initiates the **Cycle of Rejection.**

The **Cycle of Rejection** has three stages:

Stage I Birth to age seven; the groundwork is laid for our primary purpose—to matter. The three elements that contribute to this stage are parents, events, and environment.

Stage II Adolescent reinforcement based on early childhood beliefs.

Stage III Results of rejection demonstrated during adulthood.

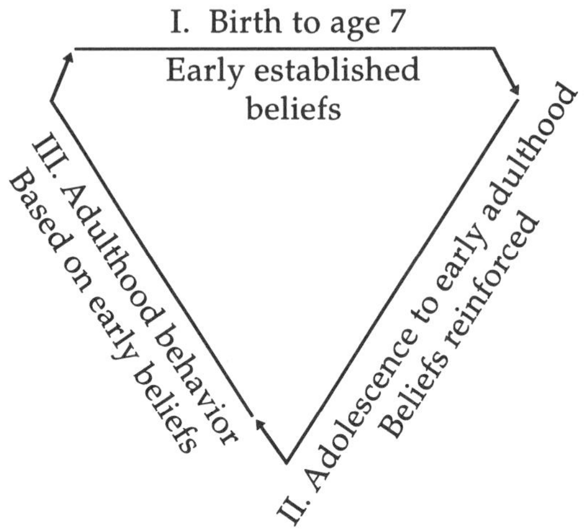

Stage I: Beliefs Established at An Early Age—Birth to Age Seven

Following are examples of how the three elements involved in this stage impact early belief systems:

Element #1: Parents

Psychological studies have shown that babies whose parents gave them loving attention, who held and nurtured them, grew to be more well-adjusted toddlers than babies who lacked similar bonding with one or both of their parents. As a child continues to grow, parents model emotions and affirm the child's expressions of emotions. When the parent acts negative, or if the parent fails to provide a balanced approach for their child's developmental dependency needs, the child may get the message that s/he does not matter.

It would be wonderful to believe that all parents could be symbolized by Mr. and Mrs. Cleaver in the old television series, "Leave it to Beaver," yet we know that the television show does not depict real life. Whether consciously or not, parents often fail to establish a belief system in their children that reinforces the child's worth. Unfortunately, the reality is that not all parents parent effectively.

Jane

Jane, today, in her forties, still holds vividly in her mind an incident that created one of her earliest memories that she might not matter. At about age four Jane failed to respond to her mother's repeated directions. "I can't even remember what it was I didn't do," Jane said. "But, apparently I didn't mind her the first or second time she told me to do something." Jane does remember what her Mother told her, "If you can't mind me and do what I say, we're going to have to take you back to where we got you." Although this comment to Jane, who had been adopted shortly after birth, was never intended to be a real threat, Jane interpreted in her mind, "If I am bad they won't want me and they'll take me back." The thoughtless comment caused Jane to question her value.

As an adult, Jane cautiously enters into relationships. She often gives much more than she gets and her close friends consider her pensive, fragile and sensitive. After her father's death, she felt compelled to be there for her mother. Although she had a life of her own several hundred miles from her mother, she spoke with her weekly and made numerous visits. She never married until after her mother's death. Although colleagues consider her brilliant (she has qualified as a Mensa), she is slow to make decisions. She either researches decisions extensively or relies on considerable input from others, an insecurity diametrically opposed to her innate capability of making decisive, intelligent decisions. Her hesitation demonstrates a fear to have her decisions questioned or rejected.

Although Jane truly mattered to her adopted Mother and Father, their lack of effective parenting skills unintentionally placed self-eroding beliefs in Jane's mind at a very early age.

Nancy with the Laughing Style

Nancy grew up in a well-to-do, East Coast family. While her father played the role of a successful businessman, Nancy says her mother actually "wore the pants."

"She'd tell my father what to do and he'd do it," Nancy says of her mother. "She ran the business with an iron hand and he stayed out of her way." The woman took the same hard line with her children, according to Nancy. "I was frequently told how stupid I was, how I'd never amount to anything, how I was simply in the way." To cope, Nancy decided to mask her pain with humor and laugh at her mother's rages. She cited the following example:

Nancy's mother had complained that Nancy didn't keep her room tidy enough. No matter what Nancy did to comply, her room was never quite perfect enough. One afternoon when Nancy returned home from a friend's house, she opened the door to her room to find that her mother had piled on the floor literally everything in her room. The curtains had been torn from the windows, the clothes pulled from the closet, everything removed from dresser drawers, even the pictures taken from the walls. All had been heaped in a pile in the center of the room. "This is what I think of your cleaning," her mother exclaimed. "Maybe after you straighten this mess up you'll know what it means to keep a room neat!" With this said, she turned and stomped down the stairs.

Nancy reacted by laughing. "I'll show you," she decided, as she walked to her bedroom window, opened it and returned to the pile on the floor. Grabbing as much as she could accumulate in her little arms, she repeated trips to the window, dropping each armful out the window to the yard below. "It became a game," said Nancy. "I laughed all the while I did it, knowing fully well I would only be in deeper trouble." Indeed she was. Nancy recalls the physical punishment following her tactics. Even more, she recalls the words her mother yelled at her: "Do you know how much I hate You? I really hate you!"

The emotions Nancy's mother modeled for her became part of her own in adult relationships. "I learned to reject people before they could reject me," Nancy admitted. "As I verbally stomped all over them, I'd laugh at their weak reactions." As the executive of a fast-growth company, she quickly learned this was not the way to motivate and inspire a productive work force.

"I now realize that I was what they, today, call an abused child," Nancy acknowledges. "I know I've offended a lot of people I cared about and created a lot of stress in my life because I didn't know how to directly deal with my childhood rejection.

Now that I know, I'm making a greater effort to treat people more humanely."

These examples may seem dramatic. In reality, they are not. Whenever I conduct a seminar or give a speech on this topic, I hear similar stories—many from women—more and more I'm beginning to hear them from men.

As children, our need to be important and matter to our parents remains insatiable. As growing, developing children, we truly need our parents to be there for us. We need to feel that we are precious and special to them. When these feelings are destroyed, we feel alone, alienated and rejected. The harsher the experiences, the more we feel rejected and the stronger a belief system becomes ingrained in our minds that we do not matter.

Element #2: Specific Events

Specific events like divorce, death, a tragic accident, a lengthy separation, such as one parent leaving to go to war or sheer abandonment, present another primary element that impacts the establishment of our beliefs. We may not always have within our power the ability to control events, yet how we deal with the people involved gives us something over which we do have control. Even in the case of divorce, where it may be an event agreed upon by both parents, the impact can be minimized if the parents deal with the children with compassion and without misplaced anger.

James

James was barely age five when his parents divorced. Although he was too young to understand at the time, he knows the custody battle must have been ugly. He remembers all the unkind things his mother and her family had to say about his father. Sometimes he even said bad things about his father himself. When he did, he said them mostly out of anger—the anger and rejection he felt for never having heard from his father after the divorce. For years, James thought his father did not love him. Why else would he have gone away and never bothered to so much as call him or send a letter? James didn't know that his mother's intense desire to hurt her ex-husband caused her to deny James' father the right to see or communicate with his son.

On several occasions when James' father had tried to send birthday or holiday greetings, his mother had intercepted.

No one ever explained things honestly to James and he grew up believing that he didn't matter to his father. "I know that in the back of my mind there were many times that I wondered what he would think of me if he knew some of my accomplishments," James said. "Like when I won a diving competition my senior year or when I got an unusually high score on my college exam.

"I'd think about how he might react. Then I'd say to myself, 'Forget it, he doesn't care, I don't matter to him'." As an adult, James constantly encountered difficulty with authority figures. Despite his good grades in college he had trouble with several professors. Despite his ability to achieve as a high producer in the field of sales, he found himself constantly at odds with his superiors. When the authority conflicted too much with his own feelings, he'd quit. He had five jobs in a span of twelve years and he always justified changing companies because someone "didn't treat him right."

James, at age 35, finally had a chance to visit with his father face-to-face and learn the truth. "Even after that, I had to constantly remind myself that I didn't have to prove anything to my father to matter to him," James said. "I still have difficulty when he tries to give me advice."

Unlike Jane, who always sought approval, James rebelled and defied authority. Both illustrate typical manifestations of feeling rejected and being out of control.

Element #3: Personal Environment

The third primary element, our personal environment, also impacts our early beliefs. The impact on children raised in the home of alcoholic parents represents the most significant environment written about today. The rejection felt by these children has been so tremendous that it gave birth to a whole movement of co-dependency. Other equally impacting environments include issues of abandonment. It took me years to realize that abandonment happens in many ways—not merely the envisioned picture we may see in a movie where a parent literally abandons a baby, leaving it on a doorstep in a basket. Here are a few ways in which children are abandoned by their parents:

- By failing to give children time, attention and direction.
- By denying and hiding "family secrets" to the outside world so that the children have to perpetuate the falsehoods in order to maintain family balance.
- Physically leaving children.
- By using children to hang on to or fix bad marriages.
- By not being there to support emotional feelings expressed by their children.
- By placing more importance on external situations like job, social and/or community involvement than is placed on time spent with their children.
- By allowing caretaker time or lavish gifts to replace personal time.
- By being physically there, yet emotionally withdrawn.
- Acknowledging pride for one or more children and none for another.

Actress Lynn Redgrave created a Tony Award-nominated one-woman play, *Shakespeare for My Father*, as the result of this last-listed abandonment issue. In an article in *Parade Magazine* she described how she felt hurt and confused by her father's coldness, an alienation that began the day she was born.

One day when her father left his diary open, Lynn discovered meticulously written details about his activities on the day that she was born. He made no mention of Lynn's birth, however. The omission, which created a deep hurt, was compounded for Lynn by the fact that her sister and brother were the acknowledged pride of their father's life. "...I was the child from whom nothing was expected," she noted. Years later, in his 1983 autobiography, *In My Mind's Eye*, her father expressed regret about his treatment of his daughter. The play became a part of her personal healing. "The play isn't just about my tragedy," Lynn said. "It was his tragedy too, that he couldn't communicate with his family. In the end, I was able to overcome it. He never did." [1]

---

[1]Michael Ryan, *I Couldn't Bear The Silence*, Parade Magazine, September 26, 1993

Richard

Richard was raised in an environment where one parent's expectations left little room to meet Richard's needs. Richard and I attended school together in Rochester, Minnesota from kindergarten through high school graduation. His father was a prominent physician at the Mayo Clinic and his expectations were that Richard would follow in his footsteps. Richard had a natural talent for music. Even as a small child I remember him playing the piano at school. He really wanted to become a musician. His father insisted he attend med-school instead. After high school, Richard was accepted at an East Coast Ivy League school. On weekends he would go to New York's Greenwich Village and play piano. Eventually Richard dropped out of college, drifting from one job to another, always talking about how he had disappointed his father. He could never live up to his father's expectations. As a result, he grew up believing that he didn't matter.

Stage II: Adolescent Reinforcement Based on Early Childhood Beliefs

When our early belief system gives a strong message that we are not valued and do not matter, each incident in our adolescent experience that reinforces the message moves the cycle forward, creating an even greater feeling of rejection and loss of control.

Because of my early childhood experiences, I related to the Hans Christian Andersen fairy tale *The Ugly Duckling*. If you recall the story, for nearly a year whenever the duckling swam out to be with the other ducks on the pond they teased and pecked and bit him until the ugly duckling flew away. It seemed that everywhere he went he was treated as an outcast. Then in the spring he saw a group of swans on a lake and decided to join them. As he swam toward the swans, he noticed his reflection in the water. What a shock to see that he too was a swan! As he swam closer to the flock of swans, they welcomed him warmly and found him to be beautiful. The ugly duckling was not really ugly, he was just different from the other ducks he tried to join in with.

Adolescence is like that in many ways. When we are different, others sometimes shun us. Sometimes they shun us from their own insecurities. Yet, if we have a belief system that says because we are different we don't belong, we allow the cycle of rejection to take control.

Remember when Miss Wenstrom told me that I would never be a secretary? Well, my early belief system allowed her message to be reinforced, that I didn't deserve, wasn't good enough, and couldn't do what I hoped to do. As a result, I believed more in Miss Wenstrom's judgments than in my own self-belief.

The more situations and circumstances that happen to us to reinforce our early beliefs, the more we will tend to lose control and carry the cycle on to our adult stage of life.

Stage III: Adult Behavior Based on Early Beliefs

In this final stage of the Cycle of Rejection, we are full-swing into denial, intellectualizing and pleasing others. While we may think that we're handling life just fine, in reality we are anything but in control. Instead we begin to mask our true feelings; we become "people pleasers"—a role particularly common among women— we deny our discomfort (denial), make excuses (intellectualize) and fantasize (stuffed feelings). By masking our true feelings we don't allow our hurt, anger or resentment to show because, if I get angry, I may not matter to you. What a vicious cycle. And, the longer we layer the masks, the more we lose control and three critical things begin to happen:

1. We disconnect from our true self, thus we often attain success, yet long for fulfillment. Nothing we accomplish seems to fill the hole—the emptiness and need for new accomplishments.

2. We connect more with "what" we are, than "who" we are; enough just never seems to be enough. More titles, more awards, more money, more things.

3. We become extremely vulnerable to taking all rejections personally. Rejections tap into the core base of our childhood beliefs and the cycle begins to repeat itself.

Taking Control Is Not Synonymous with Being Controlling

Because the business world is so competitive, I believe we often confuse "being in control" with "being controlling." Somehow we believe that if we control circumstances and people around us, we will have better control of our own lives. Not necessarily.

Generally the more controlling we are, the more we actually lose control. Take an organization that tightly controls the thinking of its people, conveying that there is no leeway for original thinking. Managers who merely reinforce this top-down thinking often find themselves with employees who merely do what they are specifically asked—no more, no less. Creativity and self-direction become stifled, productivity flattened, morale low. The more managers become demanding (controlling), the more workers become disenchanted, disagreeable and de-motivated.

Personal relationships follow similar dynamics. We are always more effective at getting what we want when we work to influence others rather than adamantly directing or telling them.

Controlling individuals have little tolerance for people who think for themselves. Thus, while managers who control others may speak of empowering employees, they rarely establish a work environment in which people feel secure enough to make decisions on their own or for which they expect to be held accountable. Instead, this controlling environment escalates the feelings of uncertainty. In effect, being controlling often backfires.

Conversely, when people feel they have some control, they become more productive and happy. People simply feel better about their work, perform better, and contribute more when they feel happy. While employers may not be able to "make" someone happy, they do have the ability to create an environment which is conducive to happiness.

My Personal Rejection Cycle

Remember, *The Ugly Duckling* as my favorite fairy tale story? I related entirely too much to the first part of the story because my early belief system told me that I was "different." I believed

I was different because that was the dominant message I heard. I heard it from my friend's parents—Alice's mother often punished me and didn't let me play with Alice because "I was different." Some neighbors treated me unkind because "I was different." Even a few of my own aunts and uncles did everything they could to let me know how different I was. When I was 19 years old I flew back to Rochester from my new home in New York to visit friends. One of the friends I specifically came to visit was Ronnie, an old boy friend who had continued to write to me. Within a few days he told me how much he had missed me and asked me to marry him. Although my feelings had waned, I was still flattered and shared the news with my aunt. "You can't marry him," she responded. "He comes from a nice family and you're different." Her message was similar to many I had heard throughout my childhood—because I was different I didn't deserve. And while I instinctively knew I was deserving, the early belief system had its hold.

Without being consciously aware of it, my adult behavior perpetuated the cycle. I played out the steps of denial, intellectualizing and fantasizing as if I were a text book case study.

When conversation with new friends and acquaintances broached the subject of childhood days, I denied any of my painful childhood, telling them instead that I had a wonderful, happy childhood (denial). I told myself that mother had not intentionally left me with my grandparents, she just had her own life to live (intellectualize). Then I'd brag about how neat it was to have had two homes—grandma's home during the school year and mom and dad's home during the summer. I rationalized my "different" situation by saying that when my executive father had to move to New York for business, he and mother decided it would be better for me to be raised in a small town where I would have a yard to play in rather than the streets of New York City. Then I'd rave about the rewards of spending each summer in New York; going to Broadway shows, shopping on Fifth Avenue, swimming in the ocean at Jones Beach. Oh, life was so wonderful with the best of two worlds. Forget the pain of abandonment (Fantasize). Year-after-year the masks would layer and the cycle continued to repeat itself. I didn't know it but the cycle was actually blocking my growth.

Results of Repeating the Cycle of Rejection

When we repeat the Cycle of Rejection it creates damaging results. It limits our potential, creates low self-esteem, causes us to feel frustrated and unfulfilled and makes us vulnerable to taking things personally. Taken to an extreme, we can even become paranoid. At minimum, it contributes to anger, depression and a feeling of unhappiness. When we carry these denied feelings inwardly over a period of time it manifests itself outwardly in such ways as feeling unfulfilled despite accomplishments, having difficulty with authority figures, and having difficulty with relationships—friends, mates, family and associates at work. As it compounds we look at ourselves as failures.

The more the cycle repeats, the more we disconnect from reality. We begin to place all our emphasis on "what" we are, forgetting the value of "who" we are. Suddenly one day we lose our job, get divorced, get denied a promotion, can't find a job equal to the status or money we once had, or any other number of rejections and we fall apart—lose face—feel unfairly treated and lose control. We feel lost, like the three little kittens who have lost their mittens and don't know where to find them; only we have lost our identify and don't know how to reclaim control of our lives.

Reclaiming control begins by reversing the Cycle of Rejection and replacing it with the **Cycle of Acceptance.**

The Cycle of Acceptance

The Cycle of Acceptance doesn't come easily; it takes dedication and work. But it's worth it. Old beliefs and habits don't die easily. Some never go away, they just fade gradually. If you think you can't reverse old beliefs, you won't. If you think you can, you will rejoice in your new thinking. And, the interesting thing about going through the renewal cycle is that sometimes we find out that some of the beliefs we held so tightly were never reality.

Mrs. Wilson's Wisdom

You may recall that Mrs. Wilson was my Girl Scout leader. She was an encourager, a friend and a true role model in my life. Yet despite my inner knowing that Mrs. Wilson believed in me, my cycle of rejection deepened to a place where I came to believe that I didn't even matter to her. As years passed by, I lumped her in with all the people I felt had failed me through the years. So, when class reunions came around, I never went. Then one year Dimi, the one friend from high school whom I had stayed in touch with, came through Dallas on a business trip with her husband. "Our 30-year high school reunion is this July," she told me. "Let's go."

I made a million excuses why I couldn't go; eventually I said, "Who would even care to see me?"

"Who cares," she said, "we'll go to see how they've done." With a little urging from my husband, I agreed to meet Dimi in Minneapolis where we would spend the night and then drive together to Rochester—about an hour away.

The Friday night reception was quite stunning; it was the first chance to see people I had not seen since graduation. Some of them would have been hard to recognize had it not been for the name tags with our high school yearbook pictures on them.

I was actually quite surprised at how many people seemed glad to see me. In my memory, I hadn't mattered to them. Suddenly one girl I had known all the way back from kindergarten, approached me with incredible excitement. She had been somewhat of an adversary through school years although we had shared the same Brownie and Girl Scout troop. "I can't believe you're here," she exclaimed. "Does Mrs. Wilson know you're here?"

"No," I responded.

"Don't call her," she demanded. "Our whole Girl Scout troop is going to have lunch with her tomorrow and you will be the surprise." I'd been called a lot of things in my life before, but rarely a "surprise." Nevertheless, I was anxious to see Mrs. Wilson and so at noon the next day I met everyone at a high rise building that Mrs. Wilson had retired to. Inside there were marble floors and large, stately marble posts. "Hide behind here," one woman said, motioning me to stand behind one of the posts.

"She'll come down to the lobby to greet us and we'll call you out for her surprise."

Quietly I stood behind the pillar—feeling rather silly and awkward. Soon I heard high heels clicking on the marble floors along with lots of laughter and chatter. Suddenly everyone became still. "Mrs. Wilson, we have a surprise for you," one of the woman said, and I was motioned to come.

As I walked toward her, she seemed smaller than I had remembered. But her face hadn't changed, merely weathered a bit with age. I sensed her surprise, like a mother in a war movie who sees her son, thinking he had been killed in the war. For a moment she stood motionless, almost as in disbelief. As I neared her I could see tears in her vivid blue eyes. Slowly she moved toward me, stretching out her arms, then hugging me ever so tightly. Gently she stepped back. Placing her hands on my cheeks to hold my face and looking directly into my eyes she said, "I always knew you'd be okay. I always knew you'd be okay" In that poignant moment I knew that I mattered to Mrs. Wilson; I had always mattered, I merely blurred my thinking when I got caught up in my Cycle of Rejection.

Perhaps you have blurred your thinking over the years. Use the Cycle of Acceptance to reshape your thinking and it will help to reshape your future. Here's how to create your Cycle of Acceptance:

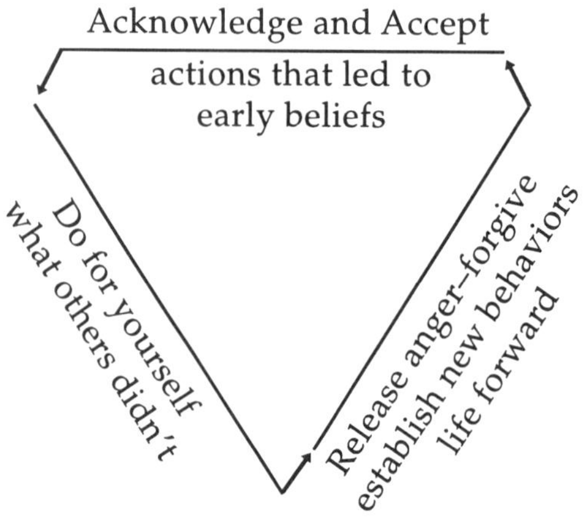

Creating the Cycle of Acceptance

Step #1 **Acknowledge and Accept.** Acknowledge the actions that led to the belief system which you established at an early age and share experiences that led to your behavior with someone you trust; sharing helps to heal and also lets us know we're not alone. Accept that it happened, recognize that it cannot be changed, look at it for what it is. Begin to explore a forgiveness process (chapter 3).

Step #2 **Do for yourself what your primary care-giver did not do.** Begin to show love for yourself. Be nice to yourself. Reward your successes, big or small. Respect yourself, give yourself credit and compliments. Believe in yourself, your worth and your value. Invest in yourself.

Step #3 **Release and Re-establish.** Release any anger, hurt or grief by reliving the experience that created the feelings in the first place. If we don't get it out, we expend negative energy keeping the lid on. Establish new behaviors; consciously think and perceive of yourself in a positive frame of mind. For example: select qualities of others that you admire and make them your own. Devote a portion of every day to complimentary confidence building. See yourself as worthy and valued through mental rehearsal (chapter 14).

By making a commitment to devote time to yourself for creating a Cycle of Acceptance, you will begin to reverse the Cycle of Rejection, taking greater control of your life and your outcomes.

CHAPTER 10

Verbal Expressions

"All bitter feelings are avoided, or at least greatly reduced by prompt face-to-face discussion"
—Walter B. Pitkin

▼ Price Point of Action 8
Master the Art of Communication

If I were forced to name only one lesson learned from my dealings with rejection and regaining control of my life, it would be to master the art of communication. Whether the issues involve personal life issues or business issues, I firmly believe that most misunderstandings, problems, disagreements and disappointments evolve from an inability to communicate effectively.

French courtier and moralist Francois Duc de La Rouchefoucauld said, "The reason why so few people are agreeable in conversation is, that each is thinking more of what he is intending to say, than of what others are saying; and we never listen when we are planning to speak."[1] All too often, I find this to be true. Thus, we think past what others are saying to us, missing the real meaning and never truly interacting in rapport-building communication. While we have been taught to speak, we have spent little time learning to listen, let alone recognizing differing styles of communication. As a result, we often spend a lot of time talking "at" each other rather than engaging in meaningful two-way communication.

---

[1]The Dictionary of Thoughts, p. 112, Doubleday, 1977

There are Four Factors that will help you to express your true self and beliefs in a rapport building manner:

1. Confront all important issues.
2. Recognize and value that there are diverse styles of communicating.
3. Learn to listen for what is not said and the underlying emotions.
4. Accept that despite all efforts, effective resolve is not always possible.

Factor #1: Confront All Important Issues

I've learned to confront certain situations, a trait some respect, others criticize. The reason I confront issues, however, is because I've come to believe that nothing can be dealt with until it is brought out in the open. It may be uncomfortable, difficult, even painful, but until you can get important issues on the table, you can't begin to effectively deal with them. Not dealing with these issues can intensify unresolved issues and, as in my case, result in years of wasted time.

About four years ago the phone rang on a Sunday morning. It was my father. He's actually my step-father; mother married him when I was two years old. Although I admired and respected him very much, I also believed that he was largely responsible for the adversarial relationship between my mother and me. In a sense, I blamed him for my not having lived with them. I thought he preferred not to have me intrude in their life. I never told him that, but I believed that.

The phone call was a total surprise since I had not communicated with either of my parents since mother had told me she had no room in her life for me — that had been about six years earlier. My father was calling, he said, because he felt that he needed to repair past damage. My mother had been very ill and hospitalized. She had improved and was back home again. Her memory was failing and her health was fragile. He felt I should know and spoke lovingly of how important it was to him that we re-establish communication. From that day forward we talked every week; the flow of communication was incredible. We eventually talked about my visiting, but he expressed concern for how mother might behave. "Are you afraid that if I come to see her, she'll reject me?" I asked candidly. "Yes," he replied. "Don't worry about that," I said, "I've dealt with that and I can handle it."

Several months later when mother took a turn for the worse, my husband and I took a plane to Florida. When I walked into her hospital room she greeted me with a bit of haughtiness, saying, "Well, well, look who's here." But it re-opened a line of communication. On the second day's visit I sat on the edge of her bed. Holding her hands, and leaning close to her, I said, "Mother, I don't know what it is I may have done to disappoint you, but I want you to know that I love you and I have forgiven you. If there's something I've done, I hope you can forgive me too." She put her arms around me and said with a rather cavalier attitude, "Oh, you haven't done anything too bad; I love you too."

It was an emotional moment for me. It didn't insure a happy ever after. But, I did feel at peace, knowing I had had the chance to bring some closure for me. And the reunion was an event that brought apparent great joy to my father and widened the door of communication for us. As we talked during the rest of my week's stay, I came to learn that it was never him who stood in the way of us being a unified family; it was always her. Her inability to express her feelings and to talk about things openly and truthfully had simply built a wall that even love could not penetrate.

When I returned to Dallas at the end of the week, I was filled with excitement and with sorrow; excited that I now had this wonderful, open line of communication with a father I had never really known and sad that so many years had been wasted with silence, secrets and fear of communicating openly and honestly.

When the issue is important — whether it's personal or professional — address it; get it out in the open; dare to confront it. Then, and only then, can dialogue begin to bring closure and resolve.

Factor #2: Recognize and Value Diverse Styles of Communicating

When I present training to help establish work teams or to build rapport through effective interpersonal communication skills, I use a behavioral profile instrument that helps individuals identify their own style of communication and recognize others' whose styles differ. It's amazing what new understanding provides in the way of opening up strong lines of communication.

One senior level executive at a major corporation I worked with had a major communication problem between himself and his secretary. He felt she asked too many questions; she felt he never gave her enough information. She accused him of being indifferent, detached, non-communicative and simply not liking her. He didn't understand what all the fuss was about. Although the two had worked together for several years and the boss always gave the secretary good reviews, she was convinced that the only reason he didn't replace her was that at her particular level, that just wasn't done without major cause. And, why hadn't she asked to be transferred or simply quit? She actually liked working for him; she just didn't think they got along very well and therefore felt frustrated.

What came out through the use of profiles was concrete information that revealed two very opposing styles of communicating. She needed lots of interaction. It was important for her to talk ideas through, to get excited about things, to make quick decisions and to express her feelings enthusiastically. He, on the other hand, preferred less talk and more to-the-point specifics. He wanted to see things in writing, take time to make decisions, gather all the facts and show little or no emotion. Getting together for weekly meetings to discuss his needs — something the secretary had frequently ask for — was not his idea of getting things done. Although they had no major work issues, the secretary was clearly frustrated. He thought everything was fine.

Since the secretary liked to verbalize everything, that's what we did. I talked to her about how he needed time to think things over; therefore when she'd go bouncing in his office with a great idea and want an immediate response, it was not his style to respond quickly. When she thought he was being unfriendly, it was merely that he didn't value talking things over; he'd rather think things over—quietly. They merely communicated differently. It had nothing to do with liking or not liking each other.

Since she was the support staff, I suggested she make the effort to adapt her style to build stronger rapport with him. The benefit would be that he would respond more readily and she would have a better feeling about getting through to him. Among the things I suggested was that she might put her ideas in writing, give them to him with time to digest at his own pace and think about. Then she could suggest a specific time to discuss his reaction. I also suggested that when she talked with him, she slow down her pace, and give him more time to hear the main points she was making. Within one week things began improving. By the end of our program the secretary had discovered a whole new person in her boss. Had he changed? No. And neither had she, she merely adapted her style of communicating with him which, in turn, eased and strengthened his communication with her.

The Four Communication Styles

There are basically four communication styles; two are more people-oriented and two are more introspective. Each of the four is motivated by different aspects. Here is what is basically unique about each:

Style 1 This style is direct; even blunt at times. They use few words, speak rapidly and tend to "tell" rather than seek lots of feedback. They may fail to listen carefully, and detail bores them — they want you to get to the bottom line.

Style 2 This style likes to talk; sometimes they talk before they think. They tend to be more subjective than objective and are generally very enthusiastic. Detail is important — it paints a fuller picture. Hand gestures are common and they are generally comfortable talking to everyone.

Style 3 This style is the silent type; not because they don't like to talk but because they want to be sure they have given everyone else time to express an opinion. They won't confront others easily — that might upset someone. They'll be careful and sensitive to use the right words and they're the least likely to "tell it like it is" without being coaxed and prodded.

Style 4 This style would prefer to put it in writing. If they have to tell you, expect them to speak slowly, deliberately and with detail. Also, expect a lot of questions — they look for solid, tangible, practical evidence. Don't waste their time — just give the facts.

Brief though this information may be, it does provide some insight into the differing styles. The important thing to remember is that each style has value. When you fail to recognize opposing styles and value the difference, you will generally encounter conflict. In order to build rapport, adapt your style to reflect more of their style.

My husband has style 3 and I have style 2. Early in our relationship he drove me nuts responding to what I thought was a simple question. First I'd have to pull a response out of him. Then it seemed like it took him forever to give me the answer. And when he did answer, I got, what seemed to me, every minute little detail. He, on the other hand, found me to be too verbose, too flowery and definitely too animated. We've come to value and respect the differences in each other's styles. Sometimes I defer to him to handle a situation because he has such a calming manner. Sometimes he defers to me because I get it done quicker. There is no right or wrong style — merely different. When we recognize and value those differences and adapt for the sake of coming to agreement on common goals and desires, we will have come a long way toward mastering the art of effective communication.

Factor #3: Learn to Listen for What Is Not Said and Identify the Underlying Emotions

Listening for what is not said and identifying the underlying emotion is particularly important when there is any stress or conflict in the communication. During strained conversations, conflict will nearly always escalate if we fail to listen beyond the words for the hidden emotion. The technical name for listening for underlying feelings is "empathic listening"— sometimes also referred to "reflective listening."

Sales people learn quickly that regardless of how practical the customer appears, when the right emotional need is met, the customer buys. There is a tremendous power connected with emotions. Antonio Damasio, a University of Iowa neurologist, asserts that emotion is central to the process of rational thought and a key element of learning and decision making. "We can't decide whom we're going to marry, what savings strategy to adopt, where to live, on the basis of reason alone," he states in a *Time* magazine article that explores the human brain.[1]

While some individuals may easily express their emotions/ feelings, other styles take a more rational approach. All, however, incorporate emotion into communication; some merely disguise it. The concept of empathic listening or reflective listening, simply urges you to listen for the feeling or emotion behind the words that are being said and reflect it back to the person you are communicating with. "Why do this?" Because if you don't, chances are you won't get to the core point of what is really being said.

Take this scenario for example: Your boss has asked you to stop what you are doing and attend a meeting that is being held in five minutes about a project you have not been involved with. He is rather abrupt and matter-of-fact. You are confused and somewhat resistant because the time will be taken away from your own deadline project. The conversation may go something like this:

Boss: I need you to attend a meeting with Jones and Smith in about five minutes.

You: What's the meeting about?

Boss: I don't have time to talk about it right now; just be there.

You: But I'm not working on anything with Jones and Smith, why do you want me in the meeting. I've got a project of my own with a deadline.

---

[1]Time, July 17, 1995, Michael D. Lemonick, Glimpses of the Mind

Boss: Don't worry about why you're suppose to be there; just be there.

Underneath the boss' adamant request that you "just be there," is an emotion that explains his abrupt, almost demanding, style. If you can identify that emotion, get it out in the open, you have a chance to create a clearer understanding, maybe even bring more clarity to the question you have. Without identifying the emotion you will most likely obey orders, go to the meeting, but be there with an "attitude."

A way in which you might have handled the scenario using the empathic or reflective communication technique would be:

Boss: I need you to attend a meeting with Jones and Smith in about five minutes.

You: Sounds like you feel pretty concerned about this meeting.

Boss: You bet I'm concerned. Jones and Smith were to have this project completed yesterday and the vice president's demanding answers.

You: And you want me to get involved at this point?

Boss: Right. I think you can help move this forward.

During times of emotional stress it is easy to simply spew dialogue back and forth without focusing on the real core issue. This technique helps to bring out the underlying emotions and feelings and helps to get the real issue out in the open so it can be dealt with more effectively. Expressing emotions and feelings when communicating negative news is also important. In the case of layoffs, communication isn't important; it's everything according to David M. Noer, author of *Healing the Wounds: Overcoming the Trauma of Layoffs and Revitalizing Downsized Organizations.* Noer likens managers communicating layoffs to presiding at a funeral. "Conducting a funeral requires an empathic touch, the naming and sharing of a feeling, and the grieving for our common human vulnerability," he writes.[2]

---

[2]As reprinted in part in *Executive Female,* July / August, 1995; p. 45. [David M. Noer, *Healing the Wounds: Overcoming the Trauma of Layoffs and Revitalizing Downsized Organizations,* Jossey-Bass, Inc.

Combining the heart and the head are not only appropriate, during difficult times, they are mandatory. Unfortunately few of us have been trained to use this communication technique skillfully. When it is used effectively, it can make a major difference in our ability to show sensitivity to others, to get along with diverse thinking individuals and to bridge differences.

Factor #4: Accept That Resolve Is Not Always Possible

The reality is that even when you skillfully communicate, some individuals won't allow rapport to be built because they would rather dominate, control and remain argumentative. At such times, you have a choice. You can choose to continue to debate a no-win, no-resolve situation or you can choose to accept that despite all positive efforts, resolve with this individual is not possible. You actually regain control when you withdraw from this type of manipulative communication tactic. Withdrawing may be the most powerful technique at this point. Withdrawing with dignity — no hostility, no shouting — no name-calling — is always an option.

I think of one specific woman who consistently tries to get her way and control every situation by refusing to entertain anyone else's opinion. She is domineering, argumentative, opinionated and down-right bossy when she confronts people with an issue she wishes to maneuver to her way of thinking. She generally begins with a calm, seemingly sensible approach. As soon as any objection or diverse thinking is brought out, she begins to employ a more dominant style. If this works easily, she simply assumes authority and begins to tell everyone what she wants done. If, instead, she encounters considerable debate, her communication tactics become directive. It becomes vividly clear that she is adamant about having things go her way. At this point, one of three things happens: she intimidates to the point that people back off and give in to her; she angers people and the debate turns to an argument; there is withdrawal with dignity.

On a recent occasion this woman confronted me in a demanding manner, expecting me to give in to her opinion that a specific volunteer project that I was in should be cancelled because it was costing too much. I tried all the effective communication techniques I knew to resolve the issue. When it became clear to me that she was not interested in resolve, but merely achieving her own hidden agenda, I withdrew with dignity by calmly making this statement: "I can't make a final decision on this based on the limited information I have heard from you. Please document the expenditures and mail them to me so I can make an informed decision and I'll get back to you." With this firm, yet non-threatening statement, I regained control of the situation. She never sent the documentation nor did she ever bring the subject up again. Remember, being controlling, does not equate to being in control.

Mastering the art of communication is like all of life's learning — it is an on-going process. As you begin to practice and use frequently effective communication techniques, they may initially seem awkward and uncomfortable. Eventually they will become second nature. When this happens you will begin to master the art of communications.

CHAPTER 11

Purple Shells

"You are here for a purpose. There is not a duplicate of you in the whole wide world; there never has been, there never will be. You were brought here now to fill a certain need. Take time to think that over."

—Leu Austin

PRINCIPLE #3

Let Passion and Purpose Be Your Ultimate Goal

What drives you? What keeps you going every day? Is it passion, purpose and a love of what you're doing? Or is it just a job?

A few years ago I found myself asking, "Is that all there is?" My business was going well, but something was missing. I couldn't be specific; I just knew I wanted something more, yet I wasn't sure what. It was one of those periods that for no specific reason I felt like I was in a rut.

It was February, a cold time in Dallas, and the National Speakers Association Winter Workshop was being held in Tampa, Florida. "Why not go to the workshop with me," I suggested to my husband, John, "and afterwards we can get a little place on the beach for a few days and regenerate ourselves." So we did. When the workshop ended we headed straight down the West coast, stopping at a cozy looking place that had beach front cabins. We called it a night early the first evening, planning to get up in time to see the early morning dawn. When we sauntered onto the beach the next morning, the warm glow of a rising sun had just begun to light up the beach. Gentle waves rolled in to kiss the sandy, white shore, leaving in their outward flow a multitude of shells. The only interruption of the early morning silence was the movement of the ocean water and an occasional "caw, caw, caw" from sea gulls flying overhead. The beach was void of the masses of humanity that would later crowd its shores. It was a peaceful, quiet moment, perfect for an early morning stroll.

Quietly we began our journey, savoring the solitude and breathing in the fresh early morning air. It was a refreshing change of pace from our normal hurried schedules. We hadn't walked too far when I began to feel a shortness of breath; my leg muscles were beginning to ache and weaken beneath me. My sedentary lifestyle was intruding on what until now had been pure pleasure.

"I think I'll have to sit down and rest," I said to John as I gave in to the tired feeling. I walked to the remains of what had once been a beautiful stone wall separating the private beach homes behind it from the public area of the beach. There I sat, trying to catch my breath and feeling somewhat embarrassed at looking back down the beach to see that I hadn't really walked very far at all. As I sat there I thought about turning back. Then I got distracted by the clusters of shells being washed to shore with each new wave. Momentarily the motion mesmerized me; then suddenly I was drawn to one particular shell. It appeared to be purple; my favorite color. I got up and picked it up. I studied it intently; it was beautiful. Cupped in the palm of my hand I marvelled at its perfect design; each tiny line flowed to meet another to create a pattern totally unique. And, indeed it was purple; deep purple on the inside, permeating through the shell to create a hint of purple that delicately tinted the outside. As I placed it in my pocket I saw another purple shell. Suddenly I had a great idea. "I think I'm ready to continue down the beach," I informed John, "and as I do, I'm going to collect purple shells."

Enthusiastically I resumed my journey. It seemed like everywhere I looked I found new purple shells. When one pocket was filled, I started filling the next. I had round shells, long shells, bumpy shells, and smooth shells. Some were thin and some were strangely structured thicker shells. All had at least a hint of purple.

When we reached a turning point I marvelled at how far we had walked; nearly two miles John estimated. Quite a jaunt for me who rarely walked or exercised. As we headed back to our cabin, I continued to collect purple shells. When my pockets became full, I created a pouch by gathering up the front of my t-shirt. When we finally arrived back at the cabin, I rushed to the kitchen sink and poured my shell collection into the basin. With the joy of a child I washed each one and carefully laid it on a towel to dry. When all were done, I stood back and proudly calculated that there must be nearly one hundred purple shells lying neatly before me. As I stood there admiring the various types, it suddenly struck me. I had walked a far greater distance than I had ever thought I would, yet I was not tired; I felt no pain; instead I felt vital, invigorated, purposeful and proud.

What had made the difference? What had changed from the earlier moments that morning when I wanted to turn back because of weakness, aching legs and shortness of breath? Then it dawned on me. The purple shells had made the difference. Deciding to collect purple shells had given purpose to my journey. Once I had a purpose and focused on that purpose, the journey became one of joy, discovery and achievement. And, although there were moments of pain and weakness, the ultimate purpose of the journey greatly diminished the momentary strain.

I think life is like that. When we focus on the pain, the temporary weaknesses and bad times, we miss the opportunity for new discoveries, new experiences, new joys. When we have a passion and a purpose, we can move beyond the pain.

When passion and purpose are our ultimate goals we can suffer temporary setbacks and pain. So I ask you, what are your purple shells? Are they dreams you have left behind? Goals yet unachieved? Relationships that have faded or love one's who have drifted from your life? Whatever they are, renew your search; claim your purple shells and collect them with a passion. You will be amazed at how much joy and accomplishment it will bring to your life, for when passion and purpose become your ultimate goal, you will regain control of your life.

I have found that there are four key issues to think about to gain clarity about our passion and purpose. What is it that you *really* want? In your own terms, what is success? Do you still trust in your dreams and what are you doing to pursue them? Finally, are you charging non-stop through life or are you stopping occasionally to create memorable moments? These are the focus of my final four Price Points of Action.

CHAPTER 12

Beware of the Doris Day Syndrome

"The people who get on in this world are the ones who get up and look for the circumstances they want, and if they can't find them, make them."

—George Bernard Shaw

▼ Price Point of Action 9

Identify What You *Really* Want

Doris Day movies were abundant when I was making early decisions about what I wanted for the rest of my life. In her movies, Doris Day was everything; a savvy businesswoman, the perfect wife, a do-it-all mother, and gorgeous to boot. I decided I'd be like her. I even wore my hair like her. Once, when we had a family portrait taken, the photographer even remarked that we looked like an ideal family taken from a Rock Hudson, Doris Day movie. Looking back years later, we did. But trying to be Doris Day was not reality. It wasn't really me and, as I found out later when I read her autobiography, it wasn't even her. It was only a series of Hollywood make-believe films.

While I think it's important to have role models, I also think it is equally as important to know and be yourself; know what you really want. I'm afraid many people go through life never knowing this. They may not consciously play the role of somebody else but, in trying to impress along their career climb, they're unconsciously patterning their behavior after someone within the organization whom they perceive to be "doing it right." Sometimes they do such a good job, they lose themselves in the process. I did that.

When my first marriage ended I joked, "Let's face it, you're not Rock Hudson and I'm not Doris Day." Yet years later, when I began to date John, the man whom I would later marry, I got a stunning revelation of just how strong the Doris Day syndrome had impacted my life.

One evening during a dinner party, a friend of John's whom I was just getting to know, said an interesting thing after we had been engaged in some lengthy conversation. "You know," she said, "you're okay. I thought I wouldn't like you because I thought you were Doris Day."

Who do people think you are? Do you convey a strong sense of yourself and do you present a clear picture of what you want and where you're going? If not, maybe it's because you're not perfectly clear about what it is you really want. You're not alone though. I meet hundreds of people each year who are frantically striving to rise to the crest of the wave. Yet when you ask the questions, *what do you really want?* the answer is often convoluted, non-specific and filled with external descriptions such as, *to be successful, to be rich, to drive a fancy car, to live on the ocean in a sprawling house with windows everywhere.* Okay, but what do you really want?

The answer to the question lies deeper than superficial answers like this. It's based in values. The specific roles—salesman, vice president, entrepreneur, engineer, doctor, lawyer, secretary, nurse, teacher—may change with different stages in our life. But the underlying purpose and passion must be congruent with one's values to be doing what you *really* want. Let's explore four core areas for identifying what you *really* want:

1. Childhood passions

2. Today's core values

3. Congruency

4. Integrity

Childhood Passions

For the past several years I have taught a course at a local community college on starting your own consulting business. As corporate America has increasingly down-sized, I am constantly amazed with the number of well-educated, talented and experienced individuals who sign up for the course. The students who enroll are generally not committed to becoming consultants; rather they are exploring the career as an option in which to use their wealth of knowledge. Few, however, envision the full transition, nor do they fully explore how to make their next career choice be one that helps them to achieve what they *really* want. One of the exercises I give them is the following:

1. Identify at least five professional characteristics and skills that you see as strengths from your most current position. Which three would be most suitable should you choose to go into this new position?
2. Identify at least five professional characteristics and skills that you see as strengths from previous positions. Which three would be most suitable should you choose to go into this new position?
3. Thinking back to age seven, what two or three things did you most enjoy doing? How do these activities tie to what you are thinking about doing?

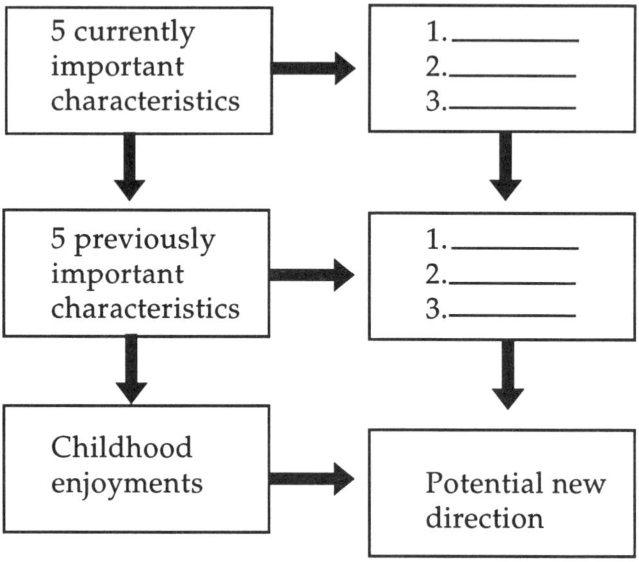

If you are going to change direction, why not make sure your new career is congruent with "who" you are as well as "what" you are so that at this point in transition you find balance in work and the rest of your life.

Men, in particular, have a difficult time with the third part of the exercise. Often they think the exercise is "childish." Heaven forbid an adult would think like a child again, a time in life when truth abounds and no qualifiers or limitations are placed on fantasies or dreams. Once they finally give in, it's amazing what light bulbs begin to go on. Sometimes I suggest that they don't complete the exercise at the moment, but take the question to bed, making it the last thing to enter their mind before going to sleep. It's amazing what the subconscious pulls up when left to work on its own through the night.

Generally I share my own experience of what I did as a seven-year-old child, or thereabout. Here are three distinctive memories:

- **Operated a grocery store.** I would ask my grandmother for empty cereal boxes, milk cartons and anything else that would constitute setting up the shelves of a grocery store. Then I ran the store, waiting on imaginary customers who I would visit with and persuade to buy lots of products so my store would be profitable. As I recall, I made lots of imaginary money.

- **Operated a travel agency.** Since I wasn't old enough to wander around town alone, I got my older cousin, Barbara, to take me to some local travel agencies where I collected numerous brochures. Back home I organized the brochures in an area of my room and sat behind a makeshift desk where I helped imaginary customers plan exciting and fun-filled trips.

- **Performed and sang.** At the drop of a hat I would perform for anyone. Before I was five, a neighbor told grandma she was impressed that I had learned to read at such an early age. I had gathered the neighborhood children together for *Golden Book* stories. I didn't really know how to read, however, I just recited the stories from memory. I also sang for school functions and played the xylophone for the Christmas pageant. I even entered talent contests and won myself an appearance on Cedric Adams Stairway to Stardom radio show, even though I couldn't sing very well.

So what does this all mean? No, not that I was destined to own a grocery or travel business or that I would be a forerunner to Madonna. There were clear indications of areas that I was naturally drawn to, however. Instead of selecting typical girl-things like being a nurse or teaching school, I chose instead to run my own business — a forerunner for becoming an entrepreneur. I also chose to perform in front of people — a forerunner for later careers, such as television, public relations, trainer and professional speaker.

When you tie together the early-childhood activities with the characteristics and skills you later used in various aspects of your professional life, you will begin to get a closer glimpse of what it is you *really* want to do.

Today's Core Values

Our values drive our behaviors. The earliest core values are established from birth to age seven, as previously discussed in the chapter on the Cycle of Rejection. Throughout life's developmental stages, various people, events and environments influence our values, thus, from time to time our values shift. Values influence the "why" behind our actions. They give continuity to decisions or actions and help formulate choices when faced with difficult decisions. Values operate on three levels: Personal, Externally-Influenced and Repressed.

Personal level values form the highest level of internal motivation because the individual feels good from "the inside out" personally from the accomplishment or success.

Externally-influenced values constitute a learned response to outside influences, such as a business philosophy or policy or a popularly-accepted measurement of success. This motivation is less long-term and meaningful. An individual may temporarily accept an externally-influenced value like being the number one salesperson (generally a monetary value), but if the personal level value is more motivated by helping people, the individual may eventually become disenchanted, even unsuccessful in the quest because the true underlying value was not being met. This is often the imbalance that creates a feeling of being unfulfilled despite succeeding.

Repressed values are those which are temporarily placed on the shelf for the sake of practicality. For example, a working journalist may secretly want to write mystery novels, but for the sake of establishing a fiscally sound foundation, works at a less satisfying form of journalism. Identifying this value is perhaps most critical for mid-life transitions when it may at last be time to do what you *really* want.

When one understands the impact of values it becomes easier to see why the happiest, most satisfied, in-control of their life people are those who come to grips with their true core values and allow passion and purpose to be the ultimate goal.

Use the following Values Clarification exercise to identify some of your core values:

Think about the definitions, then use the following scale to indicate the degree of importance that you would assign to each: **1** unimportant; **2** of little importance; **3** important; **4** very important.

Ability Usage
Make use of individual abilities.

Activity
Be busy most of the time.

Aesthetics
Be involved in studying or appreciating things of beauty, ideas, concepts, etc.

Affiliation
Be recognized as a member of specific organizations or groups.

Change and Variety
Have work which frequently changes in content and responsibility.

Compensation
Be paid well in comparison to others in similar positions.

Creativity (General)
Create new programs, ideas, structures.

Education
Continue to learn either formally or informally.

Excitement
Feel excited about my work.

Achievement
Get an accomplished feeling.

Advancement
Have advancement opportunities.

Adventure
Be involved with frequent risk-taking activities.

Artistic Creativity
Engage in creative work of various art groups.

Community
Be involved in the city where I live.

Competition
Engage in activities which test my abilities in win-lose outcomes.

Decision Making
Have the power to determine policies, procedures and courses of action.

Emotional Health
To be in a stress-free environment.

Fast Paced
Experience a constant level of activity with tight deadlines.

Friendships
Develop close personal relationships at work.

Help Society
Contribute to the betterment of all.

Influence People
Be able to influence others' attitudes or opinions.

Knowledge
Constantly pursue knowledge, truth and understanding.

Management
Plan and direct other people's work.

Parenting
Spend adequate time with my children.

Physical Challenge
Work in an environment where physical demands are rewarding.

Precision Work
Work in an environment where detail, accuracy and timeliness are rewarded.

Public Contact
Have considerable people contact on a daily basis.

Relationships
Be involved in and share in committed relationships.

Help Others
Help others in direct ways either individually or in small groups.

Independence
Determine my own direction and outcomes.

Intellectual Status
Be regarded as highly knowledgeable or an "expert" in my given field.

Location
Live in an area where I can enjoy to do the things I enjoy.

Moral Fulfillment
Feel that what I do contributes to a specific set of moral standards.

Personal Appearance
Spend adequate time, energy and money on my personal appearance.

Power and Authority
Control others' work activities; even their futures.

Profit/Gain
Work in an environment where I can accumulate large sums of money and/or material rewards.

Recognition
Be recognized visibly or publicly for the quality of my work.

Security
Be assured of employment and financial stability.

Stability
Have a predictable work routine.

Teamwork
Be an integral part of a group.

Work Alone
Work where there is little contact with others.

Working Conditions
Have comfortable work surroundings and friendly co-workers.

Religion
Being able to openly express my spiritual and religious beliefs.

Sports and Hobbies
Pursue special interests and activities.

Supervision
Have responsibility for overseeing others.

Time/Freedom
Have flexible hours and work according to my own time schedule.

Work Under Pressure
Work with time-sensitive issues and where my productivity is critically appraised.

Other/s
Values not listed that you feel are important.

Following a three-step process, determine what your five top values are and check to see if the decisions you are making in your life are congruent with your most important values. Check to see if there are any major conflicts. If you are not living a life that allows you to fully embrace your highest values, what changes might you want to make to regain control and bring your life more into balance?

***Step 1:** In the left column, list the value categories which you rated as "very important (4)." **Step 2:** In the right column, select only five from the left column that you feel are the most important of all those values you have listed. **Step 3:** As you select these five, rank them 1 - 5 in your order of importance.*

Very Important	**Top Five Values**
____________________	1.____________________
____________________	2.____________________
____________________	3.____________________
____________________	4.____________________
____________________	5.____________________
____________________	
____________________	
____________________	
____________________	

Test the validity of your choices

1. *Did you chose these values on your own and did you consider the consequences?*
2. *How much time did you give yourself before answering? Did your selections come quickly?*
3. *Will your answers meet the "Sacrificial Test?" What satisfaction will you be willing to give up to achieve this value?*
4. *Will your answers meet the "Emotional Test?" How much satisfaction or guilt will you experience when you make decisions based on these values or if you don't consider them when making decisions?*

5. *What new action will you take as a result of identifying your priority values?*

Congruency

Now that you have identified your childhood passions and today's core values, how congruent is your current career and lifestyle with your passions and values?

Susan, a long-time friend and previous business associate, worked as a graphic artist for many years, first for others, then in her own design company. She was extremely talented and often recognized with creative awards. But she encountered a period where she began to ask herself the same haunting question that I asked myself before going to Florida that one year, "Is that all there is?"

Susan loved the mountains of Colorado; whenever she could, she and her husband would visit there for skiing, hiking, horseback riding and a variety of other outdoor activities. Susan also loved fashion; she had a knack for combining separates to create smart, classy looks. And, her penchant for unusual jewelry seemed to add the finishing touch. Often she would marvel at the unique boutiques of Aspen, Vail and other artistic communities.

One year, when I had a management contract with a gift food retailer to operate their Dallas-based holiday stores, I hired Susan to manage one of the stores. It gave her an opportunity to supplement her income at a slow period in her industry and she seemed to be excited about learning something new. She had a natural talent for creating visually inviting displays. Her people skills were conducive to customer service and it was easy to see she was having fun. When the season ended Susan made a decision; she was going to close her design business, move to Colorado and pursue a new career. Her goal was to work toward owning and operating her own fashionable clothing store. It was a gutsy risk. For more than a year she endured a commuter marriage until her husband dissolved his partnership and joined her in Colorado. But she followed her dream. Today she manages a fashionable women's clothing store and is gradually building equity to take over its ownership. She has her own line of customized jewelry and designs, hand-painted clothing that is carried in specialty shops in Arizona and California in addition to her own shop. Today, Susan's lifestyle and career is congruent with her childhood passion and current values. She's much happier and fulfilled than when we shared an office together years ago and it shows. Could you make this dramatic a lifestyle change?

Integrity

Webster defines integrity as "the quality or state of being complete" as well as being of "sound moral principle; uprightness, honesty, and sincerity." In the context of identifying what you *really* want, integrity can simply be defined as being honest with yourself about what it takes to make your life whole and complete. When you are clear on this point, you will find more balance and control in the decisions that you make and it will be easier to define "success" in your own terms — the focus of the next Price Point of Action.

CHAPTER

13 Surpassing Success

"Possessions, outward successes, publicity, luxury—to me these have always been contemptible. I believe that a simple and unassuming manner of life is best for everyone, best both for the body and the mind."

—Albert Einstein

▼ Price Point of Action 10

Define Success in Your Own Terms

One of the most fascinating books I ever read on success was entitled *The Paradox of Success—When Winning at Work Means Losing at Life*, by John R. O'Neil, president of the California School of Professional Psychology. Two things stood out to me in the beginning of his book. "Their bodies go home every night, but psychologically and spiritually they remain imprisoned by the roles they have worked so hard to construct for themselves," he wrote about the trap in which many successful people find themselves.[1]

Secondly, he writes about money and its buying power being central to the meaning of success. "When our self-worth is bound to our net worth, we are condemned to living on the surface and can value ourselves only according to how others value our material success," he wrote. Thus, eventually, to remain successful in the competitive sense, "It is not enough to succeed. Others must fail."[2]

---

[1]John R. O'Neil, *The Paradox of Success*, Tarcher/Putnam, 1993; p. 24
[2]John R. O'Neil, *The Paradox of Success*, Tarcher/Putnam, 1993; p. 29.

Psychologist Abraham Maslow concluded that once the basic needs of food, shelter, and clothing are met, individuals progress to a higher level of need than money alone. Yet clearly the external trappings of monetary success are the most accepted American business measurements of success. Thus, with the downsizing of corporate America, is it any wonder that so many displaced people who once felt they were successful, suddenly feel that their lives are out of control?

A restructured work force and heightened competition have left many individuals working harder than ever and questioning the true meaning of success. *Fortune* magazine addressed this in an article several years ago entitled "Asking Too Much?" by Brian O'Reilly. "It's easy to forget that hard work is not inherently good or moral, but only as noble as what you're striving to achieve," he wrote. "Working so hard that you're a dismal parent is wrong. Working hard so you can be filthy rich is merely greedy.....Making yourself a better person—more diverse in your interests, more reflective, perhaps even more loving—may well make you a better manager."[3]

When passion and purpose become your ultimate goal, there is apt to be more balance to your measurement of success. That is not to say that monetary goals will not be important, simply that money alone does not create your yardstick.

An outplacement professional told me recently that one of the most difficult issues senior level displaced executives face, is not being able to find a position at the same monetary level. This represents the other side of success—the down side. Think of it like an ocean wave. As the wave crests, it takes us to the peak of success. But the peak of the crest is also where the wave begins its descent, so at this point, important decisions are necessary. Surfers know the strategy well; as they ride the wave to its peak, they are ever poised, ready to catch the next wave as it builds to its peak. To continue to ride the original wave destines the surfer to fall—even to be tossed around in the chaos of an undertow.

To maintain momentum, we either have to catch a new wave or take the hit. And, sometimes the new wave is less dynamic than the one before; yet it keeps us going. In life, we must some-

---

[3]*Fortune*, Asking Too Much, Brian O'Reilly, March 12, 1990; p. 46

times catch a smaller wave; we must take a step backward, to move forward and regain balance.

I remember when my husband was transferred to Kansas City. Unlike him, I had to start all over again with a job search. After checking around, I decided that I would really like to work for the convention bureau in public relations. They had no public relations manager and didn't think they needed one. Nothing I did could seem to convince them otherwise. So, I accepted an hourly-wage writing position on a part-time basis to rewrite a restaurant guide. A huge shrine convention was coming to town and the old guide was sorely out-of-date. When I finished the project the city was about to host its first big convention in a newly built convention center—the group needed help with p.r. I gladly worked with them to create press releases and arrange media appearances. Then the focus shifted to the next convention, the Republican National Convention. Media from all over the world were calling, asking for things the bureau didn't have. I got to create them. Before I knew it, a part-time hourly job had turned into a full-time management job, and the bureau finally saw a need to create a public relations manager position.

If I hadn't been willing to step back, I never would have been in a position to demonstrate a need for my talents. Did the detour diminish my success? Of course it didn't; it just created a new wave.

What are you willing to do to create new waves? Are you willing to define success in your own terms and catch a new wave that's congruent with your passion and purpose?

At different points in our life, I believe we are meant to serve different purposes. When we're balanced enough in our thinking, we can fulfill that purpose by defining and accepting success on our own terms. When we do, we are more successful in taking control of our own lives.

CHAPTER 14 Trust in Your Dreams

"See first that the design is wise and just; that ascertained, pursue it resolutely; do not for one repulse forego the purpose that you resolved to effect."

—Shakespeare

Price Point of Action 11

Trust in Your Dreams and Continually Pursue Them

Dreams do come true. It's the ability to clearly see them and pursue them that brings them to reality.

To dream is to create in your mind, life as you would like it. Once you have identified what it is you *really* want, get it clearly pictured in your mind and pursue it. I know, you're thinking, "I've heard this stuff before." But, have you tried it? The process is called many things. I prefer to use the terminology, "Mental Rehearsal." Athletes use the process routinely to perfect their performance. Why shouldn't it work just as well for you and me to enhance our lives?

The first time I consciously put Mental Rehearsal to work for me was shortly after I had moved to Dallas. I was concerned that because I knew no one I would not be able to continue being in business for myself. At the time, I was primarily doing consulting and my entire client base had been built by word of mouth. Foolishly I decided to get a job. It didn't take long to realize that I severely missed the independence of being an entrepreneur. I began to rethink my decision to get a job and, during the process I met Susan, the graphic designer I introduced you to in chapter thirteen.

Susan and I talked about sharing an office together. Our services complemented one another; I developed marketing materials and she created the art work. The only problem was that neither of us had the cash reserve to commit to an office. So we decided to apply Mental Rehearsal techniques to achieve our goal.

I pictured clearly an office high in the sky with large windows that allowed me to look out upon the beautiful sky and trees, a scene that would be conducive to energizing me with creative thoughts so that I could produce effective marketing materials for the clients I would meet. I put my mental picture into words and phrased it as though I were giving thanks for what had already happened. Each morning and night I would read the words and vividly picture them in my mind.

Within less than one month Susan called to say that Frank, a typesetter with whom she had done business over the years, was interested in the possibility of us sharing some of his office space. "What kind of rent does he want?" I asked. "We haven't talked about that," she replied, "I thought we should meet with him first."

I met Susan and we drove to Frank's office which was on Interstate 35 near downtown Dallas. It was not exactly a tower in the sky; as a matter of fact, it was only three stories tall. Frank was on the top floor. We went to his office and began to visit. Frank explained that often his clients sought his advice on many of their needs and that if he had someone like us in his office to whom he could job work out it would make his company more full service. It would benefit him, he believed, to have our talents right there in his office. Of course he wouldn't expect us to work for him exclusively, just be willing to take on his projects if he needed our talents. In other words—give us business. It all sounded too good to be true.

The practical part of me finally questioned what the cost would be. "Oh, nothing," he said, "I would just want to know you'd be available to give work to if I need it." Amazing. But not as amazing as when he walked us down the hall to view the available office. As we entered the room, I found myself looking at an entire wall of windows that allowed me to look out at the beautiful blue sky and a miniature forest of trees and greenery as beautiful as any I had pictured in my Mental Rehearsal.

For one year we shared this beautiful office with Frank and his staff. They were like a supportive family, giving us the ability to make a fresh start.

I can't tell you how it worked; but it did. I do believe that an integral part of it working, however, was that I really knew what I wanted and each morning and night when I read my affirmation and pictured it in my mind, I believed it. If you know what you really want you may be ready for Mental Rehearsal.

Whether it's Mental Rehearsal or Visualization, a term often associated in spiritual or religious environments, don't be afraid to use this powerful tool. It is used by some of the greatest achievers in a variety of fields. Dr. Mark Rogers, the anesthesiologist who, in 1987, led the team that performed the first successful surgical separation of Siamese twins joined at the head, reported later that he had visualized every step of the 22-hour operation for five months to prepare himself. Why not use this technique to prepare for your future successes?

The Mental Rehearsal Process

Pretend that you are creating your own movie script. For demonstration purposes, let's assume that you want to make a successful sales call. Just before you go to sleep at night, go through this process:

1. Picture the scenario as you would like your ideal sales call to go; see the client, see yourself walking confidently into the client's office, see the warm, receptive greeting. Say the words you would say to the client and rehearse the client's positive response, Script the entire scene with detail and picture it as an enjoyable, successful experience.

2. Picture someone you admire who does this well. If you can't think of a role model, picture an imaginary person. (At this point by having someone else in the main character point, you may feel more comfortable with the rehearsal.)

3. Pretend you are the director of this movie. Make a movie of this person doing everything the way you think it should be done to succeed.

4. Now, close your eyes and see the movie as you have scripted it. Hear the words. See the action. Feel the emotions. See the emotions on the participant's faces. If something is still not right, change it. You're the producer and director; you are in control. You can create the perfect scenario.

5. Sit back and view the movie from your directors chair until everything looks, sounds and feels just right.

6. Now, step into the part yourself; physically and emotionally. You are the part. Feel it. Be it.

7. Don't omit a single step. Now go to sleep.

8. Replay this movie for 21 days. Experience the change in your behavior and acknowledge each recognition of change by writing it down in a journal, recording the date and a brief description.

CHAPTER 15

Mr. Lewis

"Memory is the treasure-house of the mind wherein the monuments thereof are kept and preserved."

—Fuller

▼ Price Point of Action 12

Renew Your Spirit by Creating Memorable Moments for You and for Others

A few years ago, a friend of mine, who had been divorced for several years, fell in love and planned to remarry. The groom was in the prime of his life, several years older than her. She worried that her new found happiness might be threatened with a time limit because of her new love's age, so she counseled with her mother.

"Live each day to its fullest," the mother advised, "and focus on making memorable moments."

What a wonderful piece of advice, one that is worth heeding at any stage in life. Far too often there are regrets for not having taken more time from a success-driven lifestyle to create memorable moments with the important people in our lives. That's when the "if only..." thoughts set in. Why wait? Why not make time?

When I'm feeling down, it is the memorable moments that renew my spirit and help to bring my thinking into balance. I can't imagine how dreadful it would be not to have little vignettes from life to draw upon. Some are moments that were created just for me; others are moments that I created for others. Both are important, for together they fuel the passion that helps to ensure a lifelong purpose.

Memorable moments influence our future and reinforce our values. They sustain us during difficult and lonely times and inspire us during reflective times. They hide, tucked away deep in our minds and miraculously appear just when we need them.

One poignant memorable moment for me was created by a caring and gentle man named Mr. Lewis.

Mr. Lewis, in his elderly stage in life, rented a room from grandma. I remember the day he moved his stunning oak bedroom suite into the upstairs room that was to be his. He was a dignified gentleman; tall, slim, dressed in a suit, well-starched white shirt and a buttoned down vest. A gold watch chain dangled from his pocket and bounced on his leg when he walked. His thick hair was snow white and his laced black oxfords were highly buffed. He had steel blue eyes and the complexion of an Englishman, fair and barely wrinkled considering his age. And when he spoke, he totally engaged you. I knew that very first day that Mr. Lewis was going to become a very dear friend.

Soon Mr. Lewis became like a member of our family; he ate meals with us, often went on walks with us and when he took his daily walk downtown, he'd often bring back treats for us. He'd sit on the porch and watch me ride my tricycle, often commenting on how difficult it must be for me to peddle without hitting the handle bars. I had sorely outgrown the three-wheeler, but it was all I had.

One day while I was playing outside, I spotted Mr. Lewis returning home from his daily downtown trek. Beside him was a brand new, shinny, three-wheel tricycle twice as big as my old one. This dear, sweet man had determined on his own that if no one else would do anything about replacing my out-grown tricycle, then he would. And, awkward as it was, he had pulled it all the way home.

Mr. Lewis died the very next year; but his memory lives with me to this very day because of that memorable moment, a memory that supports the high value I place on building strong relationships with important people in my life.

Creating Memorable Moments For Others

While it is wonderful to look back on the memorable moments others create for us, it is even more powerful to think about the memorable moments we create for others, for it is in giving that we receive the greatest blessings. When we pass on to others, moments that they will carry deep within them, we create a legacy that will remain long after we have gone.

Here are some memories I feel good about creating for others, perhaps these recollections will help trigger thoughts of how you can create memories for others.

Memorable Moments Created for Others

My son, Blake, tells me that one of the most memorable moments I created for him was when he was very young and I made him part of a television special about amusement parks that we were filming for the television show which I co-hosted. He remembers how much fun it was to experience a bit of his mother's career by going along for the production, and how "neat" it was to later see himself on television. He says it's a childhood memory that made him feel he was able to experience something very special—sharing a work day with his mother.

My daughter, Lani, now married and a mother herself, remembers the fun birthday parties I arranged when she was a young child. One day when she told me about plans she had made for her daughter's birthday, I complimented her on her creativity, and asked, "how did you think of something like that?" "I remembered the puppet show you arranged for my birthday one year," she responded. Isn't it interesting how memorable moments get passed from one generation to the next?

As an adult business woman I have made a commitment to share my experiences with others by being a mentor. For the past few years I have been a mentor to an emerging speaker through my involvement in the local chapter of the National Speakers Association. Through the National Association of Women Business Owners, not only have I been a mentor to a start-up business owner, I have directed the local chapter mentor program. In both instances, it has been a wonderful experience. By creating memorable moments for my protegees, I feel like I am contributing to their growth in a unique way. The incredible thing is, while I'm mentoring them, I get so much in return—their fresh perspective, their enthusiasm and the opportunity of seeing things through their eyes.

I took the liberty of asking my protegees what memorable moments they thought I had created for them. From their perspective, I share their responses with you.

Dianne—Tomorrow's Top Marketing Guru

Dianne attended a marketing workshop that I presented for emerging businesses. "Here I was, with 13 years of sales and marketing experience, and I was hearing things in your seminar that I needed to hear in order to run a successful company," Dianne recalled. "I went home from the workshop so excited to tell my husband about the program. I also told him that during the workshop, it dawned on me that I needed a mentor just like Bette Price. "

Coincidentally, it was no more than one week later when Dianne had a luncheon meeting with another business woman whom, when she found out what Dianne was trying to accomplish, told Dianne she needed to see if Bette Price would be her mentor. "That did it," Dianne said, "I called you and asked if you would meet with me. When you did, and I asked you to be my mentor, you agreed.

Dianne recalled a specific time she came to me for advice, as being a memorable moment for her. We met to discuss how she might salvage a proposal that she had spent considerable time preparing for. During the presentation, the prospective client had challenged her unmercifully, pushing for step-by-step marketing tactics that he had no right to expect in proposal form. She had held her own, yet she wanted some feedback about how she had handled the situation, as well as some advice on how to handle revised strategy when she went back to the client.

"You just focused in on everything I needed to deal with," she recalled. "You evaluated what I had done right, what was inappropriate on the prospects part, how to address it professionally and how to approach the next meeting. I needed that honesty and experience."

In a brief time I have developed such a close relationship with Dianne that I think of her much as I would my own daughter if she were starting out on her own entrepreneurial venture. It's a wonderful feeling to know that this capable, talented young woman, who would no doubt have made it fine without me, will nevertheless feel a little better about her growth for my having been there for her.

Eloise—Poised for Creating Momentum

My formal mentor relationship with Eloise is about to come to an end, yet I will no doubt continue to work with her informally. We have been through a lot—from developing marketing materials to my being there to hear her do a 15-minute showcase. She is well on her way to making a full-time profession of helping others to create momentum in their lives—the thrust of her programs. There is little doubt that she has what it takes to deliver high content, highly motivating presentations.

When we began our mentor relationship, Eloise was thirsty for guidance. She recalled that I laid the groundwork early for how I would provide that guidance. "I will not tell you something just to be nice; I'll tell you the truth based on what I believe, what I've experienced and what I think will help you grow," Eloise said I told her during our first meeting. "Throughout the year, you questioned me about decisions and really made me think."

One memorable moment Eloise recalled having meant the most to her, was when I pulled her aside after a 15-minute showcase presentation she made to the mentor group. "You gave me honest feedback and said some very positive things," Eloise recalled. "Because you had prefaced our relationship with honesty, I knew you would not have said those things if you had not meant them. I felt so excited about your feedback, and I said to myself, 'I can do this!'."

It's a wonderful feeling to know that you have created memorable moments for others. Not that they are major, life-changing issues, but that the moments were important enough to contribute to the development of another person's life. What a legacy.

What memorable moments have you created for others to help support their values, passions and purpose?

Life is short. Make the most of it. Don't wait for tomorrow to begin making memorable moments for you and for others. What memorable moment can you create today?

CHAPTER 16

Please Don't Eat the Pages

The great end of life is not knowledge but action.

—Thomas Huxley

One of my favorite sayings is an anonymous one: ***You buy them books and buy them books and all they do is eat the pages.***

PLEASE.....don't eat the pages!

If there is anything of value you have learned from this book, please put it to action in your own life. It is less important to implement each and every Price Point of Action than it is to seriously commit to one point and get started. Once you begin to see results in that area, begin work on the next. Remember, regaining control of your life is a process, it doesn't happen overnight. However, nothing will ever change if you don't take that first step.

Here are a few final thoughts to help you take action:

▼ **Talk about the actions you plan to take.** Talking helps to process things in your mind and get your fears, concerns and other feelings out in the open. While you will be in charge of the actions you chose to make, it is difficult to do it all alone.

  Develop a support system of people you can talk to when you're getting started and when it seems tough to see the light at the end of the tunnel. Select people you trust, who will challenge you if need be, but who will also understand that sometimes all you want is a friendly ear to listen.

- **Make YOU a priority.** You can't move forward if you don't leave any time to make the moves.
- **Investigate options of possible help.** Be willing to reach out and ask for help when you think you might be stuck. There are many resources if you look for them.
- **Be inquisitive—seek new information.** No one book will be a cure-all. There are many worthwhile books on the market to foster thinking—some new, some written years ago. Napolean Hill's *Think and Grow Rich,* for example, is as valid today as when it was written. Each individual has a different "ready status." Timing is everything. You may have read something in this book that you read in some other book previously, yet because of your "readiness factor," the information was more meaningful this time. The more viewpoints you expose yourself to, the more able you will be to make choices.
- **Document your progress.** Begin a journal and write down significant actions and results. Emphasize the positive things that happen each day. During a particularly difficult time in my life, I challenged myself to find something positive to write down each day. This helped me to focus on the resolves, rather than the problems.
- **Think creatively.** When faced with decisions, think of several ways to make the decision. There is always more than one way to tackle a situation—write down all possible approaches, then evaluate the consequences of each. Select the decision which results in consequences most acceptable to you.
- **Feel your feelings.** Become aware of the feelings that lie beneath your words and actions. Take time to identify what past history may have triggered the feelings, then evaluate the intensity of the feelings. Ask yourself, "am I overreacting to this situation because of past history or does the situation deserve this amount of intensity I'm feeling?" Be as honest and objective as possible. If you realize you have overreacted, calm down and rethink the emotional reaction. Put things in a new perspective. As you continue to process your feelings in this manner, you

will find that you begin to have a better understanding of your immediate reactions, thus a stronger ability to regain control of your emotions.

- **Listen intently.** Practice setting aside emotions during critical decision-making conversations. Let the facts drive your response, not the emotion.
- **Think positively.** As trite as this may sound, those who think they can, can. Those who think they can't, can't. Be a proactive, positive thinker.
- **Reward yourself.** Find small ways to reward yourself for using good coping skills and for growing in your ability to take control of your life. Create "reward coupons," listing on each coupon one thing that you would consider a treat. List things like, go to a movie, take a bubble bath, get a massage, play golf, eat an ice cream cone, read a mystery. Put all the coupons in an attractive box. When you recognize that you deserve a reward, open the box and pull one out. Then, go do it.
- **Remain flexible.** Remember that the wings on the aircraft that crashed, broke because they lacked enough flexibility. When your thinking becomes rigid, you mentally put yourself in a similar position. Learn to be flexible, embrace change as new opportunity. Give new ways a try.
- **Release anger.** Get to the base of your anger. Identify the core feeling that manifested itself as anger. Understand it, feel it temporarily, then let it go.
- **Refuse to be victimized.** Through circumstances you may become a victim, yet you do not have to allow yourself to be victimized—destroyed. It is your coping skills that will allow you to control what the result of being a victim will be.
- **Never stop learning.** My friend, and colleague, Joe Charbonneau, says you're either ripe and rotten or green and growing. Keep green.
- **Share.** Once you learn something new, share it with others, pass it around. Competition can be healthy as long

as it doesn't dominate your actions. There is much more power in sharing—there really is enough to go around.

- **Smile.** As simple as it sounds, look around—how many people do you see smiling? When you smile, you encourage others to do the same. When you smile, it makes it nearly impossible to sound grumpy so it helps to add a smile to your voice as well.

- **Laugh.** Laughing is good for your health. Find something funny in every day. Strengthen your sense of humor. Take a humor workshop, rent a humorous movie, hang around with funny people.

- **Love.** Take plenty of time to demonstrate your love to others. In looking back over my own life and questioning what contributed to my taking the high road rather than the low road, I concluded it was love. Despite my difficult childhood, I was loved. I truly believe that love was the underlying core element that enabled me to turn my life around and begin to live life forward. With love, many things are possible.

Please, please don't eat the pages of this book. Begin to take action. And as you begin to experience success with your personal journey of regaining control of your life, add to this list. Write me about your positive experiences, I'd love to share them in my next book, or fax your stories to me @ 214-980-2302.

Good luck!

Author's Note

If you have found the contents of this book helpful, inspiring, or thought-provoking in helping you to make some positive changes in your life, I would very much like you to feel free to write or fax me personally and share your experience.

If you would like to be kept informed about future books and other publications or upcoming seminars, I will be happy to add you to my mailing list.

If you are aware of an organization or group that you think would benefit from having me provide a keynote speech or seminar based on this book, please contact me:

Bette Price
The Price Group
4151 Belt Line Road, #124-223
Dallas, Texas 75244
Call: 214-404-0787
FAX: 214-980-2302